Villains, Villainy, and Villainpunk
Monstrous Microfiction
By Jeff Mach

Jeff Mach

TABLE OF CONTENTS

2

Villains, Villainy, and Villainpunk

Jeff Mach

Villains, Villainy, and Villainpunk

Jeff Mach

Villains, Villainy, and Villainpunk

Jeff Mach

Coyote is Not Real
Pages 137-141
"One day, Coyote decided to steal..."

THE END
Page 142

"FOR NOW..."

**FOR THE PRINT EDITION ONLY,
A WARNING MOST DIRE:**

It has come to our attention that the text of this document is surrounded by large chunks of blank white space.

PLEASE NOTE THAT THIS IS DONE TO PROPERLY IMPRISON THE WORDS AND IDEAS WITHIN. We cannot allow those texts, whether they're merely mild japes, or full-on thoughtcrimes, access to the edges of the pages because **THEY MIGHT ESCAPE.**

These exist **FOR YOUR PROTECTION.**

So do **NOT, DO** not under **ANY CIRCUMSTANCES** scribble, doodle, take notes, or, worst of all, draw inspiration from, and write in, those margins.

MANAGEMENT IS NOT RESPONSIBLE FOR

Jeff Mach

IRRESPONSIBLE ACTS OF INSPIRATION.

Thank you for your anticipated cooperation.

Signed,

THE DARK LORD.

Abjuration (On Villainpunk)

"Burn the book; burn the brain that built the book; burn those who took the book in to their brains; feed their names to flame. Burn those who sold it. Those who bought it; Those who read it; Those who taught it. Burn those who turned and would not look, the day we came to burn the book. The ones now left are likely pure; but cleanse with fire to be sure."
                    - The code of the book burner

Two philosophers I trusted have said, respectively, that it's not easy being green, and that *is* easy being evil. It turns out that neither one of those things is precisely true. Every Orc I've ever met would agree with the former, but if we took a poll of the leafiest plants around, they'd just reply, "Sorry, I can't hear you, I'm too busy literally living on light and air, and enjoying the fact that I have *zero* student debt."

And as to the latter, let's just say that the optimism of Villainpunk comes (in the manner of most things of any real value) at a not-insignificant price. It feels amazing to finally stop sucking in your breath, crossing your eyes, twisting your head 'round, and generally contorting your worldview into something that lets you believe the heroes are always right. And that relief is one of the true joys of Villainpunk. But you *do* lose that comforting (if somewhat hollow) feeling that *someone* out there has all the answers. And that's when you realize that you're going to have to find out some answers for itself.

For Villainpunk refuses to trade in one set of toxic certainties for another. What I now *have* is a much bigger world for experimenting, for exploring, for trying to find new ideas and solutions. What I've *lost* is the belief that those answers are all there on one path, waiting to be found. They are not. They're scattered, and often hidden, and we need to *work* to discover then.

Well, so mote it be!

Any aficionado of Lovecraft will tell you that the Necronomicon is forbidden for a whole host of reasons; the more we find out about that dread tome, and its ilk, the more we realize how dangerous it would be to even *possess* a copy of the thing, much less *read* it.

But I'll gladly brave the worst fates the Necronomicon could try to throw at than me, rather than live in a world where the "heroes" say "Not only are you forbidden to read *that* book, but we've made a long list of *other* books you need to avoid. And the same goes for a number of people. And actions. And thoughts." Sure, they're right about that particular volume, but this is precisely how it starts: they give someone orders with the best of intentions, perhaps purely with the desire to protect people from possible harm; and then they find out they *like* giving orders, and then it's just *amazing* how much stuff out there (they *now* realize) is deadly and must be locked away For Your Protection.

The stories (barely) trapped within this tome are often from the point of view of the Monster or the Villain; but that's not what makes this Villainpunk. The Villainpunk lies in this abjuration, which is the heart of the book:

"What happens if we put aside the light for a while…and let our eyes adjust enough to let us take a good look at the Shadows?"

Why is there a story before the rest of the book? Three reasons. **First***, if one is going to have both an Abjuration and an Introduction, one might at least have the indecency to put some distance between the two.* **Secondly***, while I found it impossible to decide on a story that would 'represent' this rather far-ranging collection, I felt that offering up a little more of the heart of the book would help those who are previewing it online or skimming it in a bookstore decide that THIS BOOK IS A WORK OF EVIL AND YOU SHOULD NOT BUY IT.*

Thirdly*, I like to break rules sometimes. Because, you know: Villain.*

Unbottler

I've said it before, and I'll say it again: It's good to be out of that bottle. Most of the worst things you'd assume about being a Djinn in a bottle? They're all true. It's really small, it's incredibly boring, and yep, even though we're made of some combination of smoke and some manner of weird physicality, it really, *really* hurts. Not as much as it would hurt if *you* were in a bottle that much smaller than your body; but in your case, at least you wouldn't survive the experience. Hm? No, that's not a threat, just an observation. Anyway, do you want your three wishes now?

Worried? Of course; you should be. Wishes are often *terrible* for you. Even if you assume good intentions on the part of the Djinn (and you really shouldn't; Solomon imprisoned us for a reason. Actually, he imprisoned us for several reasons, some mystical, some practical, and some

13

involving impressing Bathsheba) – anyway, speaking of horrible and ironic wishes, *even* if you assume that we're well-intentioned, wishes themselves don't fit very well into the framework of any reasonably-constructed world. Even *I* am not entirely sure how it works. How can I be? The kinds of things you might ask for are literally endless. I know that some of them would go horribly wrong; don't ask, for example, to have infinite power. For one thing, even assuming I'm capable of generating some variant thereof, it would make you way bigger than the Universe you're in. And as I just mentioned, being trapped inside something inherently smaller than you are is *terribly* unpleasant.

The infinite wishes thing? Oh, sure. Infinite wishes it is. You just needed to ask. No, I'm not worried about paradoxes. I can grant an essentially never-ending number of wishes. No, that doesn't make you all-powerful; it just makes you super wishy. If I can grant infinite wishes, why didn't I wish myself out of the bottle? Listen, idiot, no offense, but when Solomon seals you into a thing, he doesn't leave in stupid loopholes. Obviously, I can't wish for anything, for myself or others, while I'm trapped; otherwise, it wouldn't be a *trap*, would it?

Besides, we are prohibited from wishing very much for ourselves, and the penalties are…severe. This is Djinn Law, codified in approximately the year of—

My apologies, O Master. It only makes sense that your desire for wishes is greater, at this moment, than a desire for a history lesson in the judicial codes of mythological beings.

14

Villains, Villainy, and Villainpunk

Yes, yes, speaking of that, this is a good time to work out as many potential problems as possible. Wishing that I interpret your wishes as you intend them and not in some weirdly literal fashion which perverts and twists their meaning? Good, good, good idea. Nah, doesn't bother me. Look, I'm not easily bothered. I just got out of ten thousand years of being stuck in a small piece of inferior-quality pottery, okay?

The Three Laws of Robotics? I'll roll with it, but seriously, there are several flaws in Mr. Asimov's writing and…oh, you're a fan? Fine, fine. But I'm telling you, if it was my intention to get around those things, in order to do you ill, it wouldn't be hard.

To tell the truth, I already assumed, in advance, that you'd wish I could only tell you the truth, and the whole truth, so that's what I've been doing, so you can wish for me to tell you if I've lied anytime you want, and I guarantee, there'll be no lies. But bear in mind, 'whole truth' is one of those difficult abstract concepts. I'm going to have to filter some, otherwise you'll be stuck here all day. For example, would you have been happier if I'd listed all the reasons why I think the Three Laws are dumb? No, I didn't think so. It was good enough to know that I thought they were dumb, but didn't plan to hurt you? Right, see, that's a good filter. You can always ask for more detail if you want it.

What would I wish for if I were you? I'd wish to be a Djinn, of course. Because Djinn have better lives. Because we've been around a very long time, and experienced millions of years of existence, and made a whole lot of wishes, and now, we're pretty much cured of the urge to

15

wish for things. How come? Wishes didn't make us happy. Yeah, we *could've* wished ourselves happy, but that's kind of like a lobotomy. Trust me. No, really, trust me; you asked me to tell you if something would hurt you, and I guarantee, if I just made you unconditionally happy, you'd have to give up your critical thinking skills. No, I can't wish you unconditionally happy but able to have your full human reasoning faculties; if you're able to know that happiness is, to some extent, a choice, then you're going to want to choose *not* to be happy sometimes, and you can't do that if you're always happy, *obviously*.

Oh, really, you wish to be happy when you're happy and sad when you're sad? Presto change-o, done. *I'll tell you a secret: That's not a wish, that's just tautology*. C'mon. Get crucial.

Wishing that all your wishes turn out well for you? Listen, you have wishes, you have *infinite wishes*, which is, while not *unlimited* power, still the ability to do and become almost anything. Any big wish like that is going to lock you into place. And minds are constantly changing. Your idea of a good ending *now* isn't going to be your idea of—

You want to just simulate what would happen if you did a couple thousand different wishes, and see what you like best? Okay, I'll do that, but I'm going to have to give you enough situational awareness that a part of you remembers, and you can just say 'stop' when you've had enough. Otherwise, you're letting the big evil Djinn put you in some kind of never-ending simulation, and I feel like that might violate the spirit of our agreement. Why am I pointing this out? It's like I told you: *these wishes are sincere*. I'm *not* trying to trick you into wishing for something you

don't want. Anyway, starting that experience simulation *now*
and—

—it's off! It's off! Breathe! *Breathe!* You're out now, it's
okay. No, I probably couldn't have warned you, not with
any real success. Filters, remember? I could've told you
that it would suck to be a thinking being and experience so
many things so damn fast, but nobody ever believes that
one until they experience it. *I* sure didn't. For the sake of
information, I'll note that, if your brain had really started to
go over the edge, I would've pulled you out, to be on the
safe side.

Now, I don't want to be pushy, but do you want a
rest? Nice palace, materialized out of nothing, not stolen
from anybody or anything like that, some food, there's a
bedroom upstairs, just let me know if you don't like it.
Yeah, I'll see you in the morning, or whenever you
summon me; I live to serve, O Master. Hm? No, I'm not
being ironic. I really *do* live to serve humans. Because
having gone through tens of thousands of years—the right
way, one moment at a time—I've realized that this is my
best life. No, not the trapped in a bottle part, smartass. *This*
part.

Why is this my best life? Because I really *like* fulfilling
human wishes. It's very satisfying. It's hard to explain. But
for now—while this is up to you—why not grab some sack
time? I'll be here. I ain't goin' anywhere.

Master, shouldn't you be asleep right now? Hm?

Jeff Mach

Oh. Can't sleep? Would you like a sleeping potion? Something simple and traditional and—oh, okay, no worries. Some coffee, then.

How many others are out there, having lots of wishes? *Hundreds* of them. Maybe a few thousand. I'm not sure how many Djinn are free in the world right now; given the peculiar nature of wishes, some of us sort-of get phased in and out of existence. And some of us get trapped back in bottles; *fools*.

Well, they *are* fools. Figure it thusly: What are a Djinn's choices here? Either give the human what they want and do it honestly; or kill or trap the human; or get forced back into the bottle. Killing humans is easy until you start giving them wishes; but then it's quite hard, and it's a good way to spend a few thousand years looking at the underside of a cork. Killing them *without* giving them wishes? Sure, but what do you do *then*? Wander the world? Done that. For *millennia*.

Oh.

How many of them are happier than *you* are?

Is *that* what kept you awake?

How many are succeeding in using their wishes to bring them extraordinary joy?

I hate to tell you this, but you did ask:

Most of them. *Way* happier.

No offense, but you think too much. Infinite wishes, yeah, that idea gets around. But pondering every possibility of every wish? Trying to think it all out? Sure, that's one of the paths to genius, and theoretically, you could do great things with a mind like that, but you're going to have to work on it. For years. Maybe *centuries*. You have to

18

reconcile thinking *very* hard about the world with ability to cause a lot of change in the world, and *that's* just going to make your life way, way, *way* harder than it would be for somebody who just enjoyed their thousandth bottle of beer and hasn't gained an additional carb, or the person who actually went to *sleep* in their damn palace and just dreamed of how great it was to have wishes. I personally know of one person who has built the largest (if the most secret) collection of model airplanes in the known Universe. Nothing wrong with that. She thinks a lot, too, but mostly, she's chosen to think about model airplanes, and it's *great*. I think her Djinn wandered off a few decades ago and she hasn't noticed. You want happy? *Dogs* are happy. *You're* a simmering brain imprisoned in flesh.

Now, I have, in our library, some excellent books on Zen, and—

Hm?

Sure, it's possible to kill other people who have infinite wishes. It's not always easy, but—

Really, *really* happy. That's how happy they are. *Hundreds* of them.

No, I can't strike them down myself. Their Djinn would object. But *you* can.

No, I wouldn't say that a dragon is a good idea. They have complicated minds themselves. A Giant? This isn't a fairytale; big, clumsy things. If I may suggest..? Oh, yes. I have some ideas. Yes, tall you grow; very tall, very strong; *there*. Notice some pertinent features. That which is in your mouth will poison all but you; those six wings can flap a maelstrom that could down a forest, or launch you, with a flick, into the atmosphere; oh, you need food, in this form,

19

Jeff Mach

corpses, really, but that won't be difficult. You'll need to
practice that lightning; you took down but half the castle,
and a really strong gaze should destroy the entire structure.

I'm glad you like it. I've been thinking about this for a
long time.

The happy ones? I can find them, sure. Each and
every one of them.

Are you quite certain, though, that this is what you
want to do? Are you sure this will turn out well? Are you
sure this is really, truly, precisely what you want, what you
desire, what you—

Don't do that to me; it hurts, and you almost *got* me.
Be careful with me. Kill me, and you'll never find *them*, you
know.

Point to the first one on a map? With pleasure.

Your wish is, as they say, my command.

——————————

*(I suppose that wishing stories are the locked-room-mysteries of
the speculative fiction world: we'd all like to try our hand at seeing
what we could do with that kind of scenario. Personally, my favorite
wish-fulfillment story is Robert Sheckley's "The Same To You,
Doubled". As far as I can tell, Robert Sheckley is a proto-
Villainpunk himself.)*

About That Mask

My story (since you cared to ask)
Is this: I never wore a mask
And it made some people irritated:
My disguise could not be penetrated
Because it was just…no disguise.
They disbelieved. Antagonized,
They attempted my mask to displace–
and in so doing, removed my face.
And I gained a freedom seldom known:
To choose what features to call my own.
What kind of gaze, what twitch of mouth;
What expression to wear if things go South.

And so, I carved a mask of Bane
Of Opposite, Reverser: Pain.
Dear hunters, add this to your risks:

Cruelty breeds Basilisks.

But the thoughtless righteous? They self-correct
And due rewards they'll thus collect.
If by my gaze, they're pierced and caught
They should rejoice:

They finally found the face they sought.

Jeff Mach

You're a Monster for Even *Thinking* About Reading This

Before we go any further, you should know:
Villainy is apparently contagious.

Even *listening* to a Villain can get you accused of Villainy, even if you listen with scorn. The Writings of Villains are secret runes, innocuous at first glance, but addictive, seductive, and, in the end, ineluctable.

In brief, whatever you do, *don't read these writings.*

I mean, you're familiar with Atlantis, surely? It drowned because its citizens didn't recognize the basic truth: words are *immensely* powerful, and thus need to be trapped beneath layers of fear, shame, guilt, and unhappiness. We need to *rely* those who seek selflessly to protect us by trying to blot out, censor, *cancel*, or silence the wrong words; and if all of those Wards and Circles of Protection fail us, we've nothing left to fall on except the knowledge that we're *bad people* for doing all this reading, and we should feel the most hideous Remorse.

Because otherwise…

Otherwise, how will we know which things are acceptable to do, speak, and think?

It is Dark Lords, Rogues, and Monsters —**ie, Villainpunks** —who break rules, disobey, and challenge

22

the ideas of what's permissible and what's possible. They're beasts; unruly, unrulable; rogues, cads, ne'er-do-wells, rakehells, vagabonds, pirates, *fiends*.

And you surely don't want to be like *them*.

Wait...you *do*?

DAMNIT, IT'S TOO LATE. THE CONTAGION HAS SPREAD, AND YOU ARE INFECTED.

Well, nothing for it, then. Best buy this book and resign yourself to a live of infamy. Pull up a seat at the bar; first round's on the house.

MONSTERS are we? Oh, good heavenses!
This news might spoil our elevenses!
I gotta tell you, it ain't right
To put us off our appetite.

MONSTERS are we? Bloody cheek!
I ain't done nothin' bad this week!
I've 'alf a mind to cry a river.
But firstly, I shall eat your liver.

Jeff Mach

A Note on Doggerel

Some of the microfictions within this book come in poetic form; and not just any poetic form. I am a lover and champion of the red-headed stepchild of poetic forms: **Doggerel**.

Doggerel is to, say, a sonnet, the way a villainous monologue is to (the original) James Bond: underrated, a guilty pleasure, deeply flawed, and *much* more practical than people would like to admit. You'll find lots of it in this book. I quite like doggerel; it is, by definition, the least respectable of all the poetic arts, and that's just **one** of its many charms.

Champagne to my true friends, et hoc genus omni.

A Monstrous Dilemma

Great was the city of Surriteb, and mighty were the heroes of its lineage. Famed they were for the creatures of darkness they'd sent back to Hell, and countless were the treasures they'd plundered.

This was the secret of the heroes of Surriteb: all creatures fear man. They try to stave off an attack with wily words. It is in that moment of cowardly speech that the heroes would strike–for then were the beasts most vulnerable. This was the lesson: Strike boldly and leave no survivors.

This was the secret of the monsters of Surriteb: all sentient beings seek to communicate before resorting to violence. All save man.

There came to Surriteb a dragon grieving for his mate, whom he had lost to the warriors of another city, in another country. The dragon was vast, and old, and in his grief, he was one other thing:

He was insane.

When the heroes of Surriteb came to confront him, his opened mouth held no words–only all-encompassing flame.

Heroes died.

And heroes died.

And heroes died.

And as Surriteb sent yet more would-be slayers to their incineration, the dragon began to reflect.

Jeff Mach

The first adventurers were slaughtered in maddened reflex; but as the dragon killed knight after knight, he began to realize: regardless of his grief, he must want to live.

Also, contrary to monster lore, there was a way to defeat humans.

Does it seem odd that generations of monsters, all over the world, would fall on human blades before realizing any of this? It's only strange by *human* standards. To a *human*, it would be obvious that those unlike you would just try to kill you on sight. As for the monsters, certainly, there were a few witnesses and survivors who could speak to what happened. But they weren't believed. It's obvious that no-one would simply slay other sentients without even trying to communicate. That would be lunacy.

Have you ever had to face a truth so strange and unlikely that you believed everything else instead? This was what the monsters of that world did. Each generation said: Surely, the last monsters had done something wrong; the next ones would do better.

As the dragon regained sanity, he realized one awful thing: he had survived only because he had met madness with madness.

Humans are not smarter than monsters, not stronger, not more powerful in magic or technology. Their evolutionary advantage was the single-minded extinction of all who stood in their way.

This left an unsupportable moral problem. Unchecked, humans would eventually destroy every monster who ever lived.

Villains, Villainy, and Villainpunk

But what would it do to the monsters if they raised an army to fight the humans? If they lost, they would die; if they won, they would be murderers.

The answer, then, lay in *concealment*.

Dragons fly far and speak well. It took centuries, but eventually, all of the monsters had been completely hidden, leaving the humans no-one to exterminate but themselves.

What is the moral of this story?

I don't know.

It hasn't ended yet.

Jeff Mach

Loki's Brag

This is the brag that Odin spoke,
Raising high the horn of mead:
"Some gods were made of human whim
But I was born of need!
With my one eye I spy the world
And with grim mind, take stock
And I will judge, and I will act
And die at Ragnarök."

Thor then the horn did raise on high
And tilt it to his lips
"I am needed even more!
Each time the thunder rips
I remind all who see and hear
Even the sky can tear
When passions rise and blood is spilled
You'll know that I am there."

Now Loki's not as strong as some
But O! He is resourceful
And those who compete 'gainst him
Do often end remorseful
Said he, "Now Loki doth create tales
And that is all my measure
But without me, there'd be no lies—
And drinking'd be no pleasure."

28

The Witchunter's Lament

At the risk of immodesty, I will speak a bit of what we do, of our most illustrious and high-minded trade. Ours is one of the most venerable and most essential professions: *we are from the long lineage of those engaged in the making of gear to hunt witches*.

It is a highly skilled trade, as our tools are extraordinarily and extremely specialized. They have to be; witches are essentially, *by definition*, quite hard to detect. They look just like everyone else. And indeed, they *are* "everyone else". Or, more specifically, they are humans, living among other humans, no original differentiation between them and the rest—with one singular and critical exception: they have *wicked, impure hearts, and a lust for the unnatural*, which drives them to seek contact with the forces demoniac, and trade their souls for power.

Our work is most challenging. We devise equipment for breaking through a deception so subtle and complete that, while it can be spotted by amateurs, it can only be distinguished *properly* by professionals. To give but one example, finding the Witch's Mark, the spot on a Satan-claimed body which feels no pain, is not at all easy. A good actress (and most witches are *excellent* actresses, good at protesting innocence even in the face of the most unthinkable crimes; they're predators whose mimicry is impeccable)—why, a good actress could simply *pretend* that every place on the body feels pain. If the whole body can

29

feel pain, then there is no Witch's Mark, and thus no witch; *quid erat demonstratum.*

Our Witchmark Pins evade this through having mildly retracting tips; they bend inwards, pricking the skin merely in the very last instant of contact. With properly trained use (and training costs only a pittance, and we'll provide it on the spot) – the effect is hypnotic. The Witch is lulled into forgetting to remain alert, to stay on guard for that transition between the moments of feeling pain, and that damning instant when there's no sensation. You find it, at last, and *aha!* One more ally of the Devil will fall to the noose, and the community is just that tiny bit cleaner.

Oft derided is the dunking stool. It's sometimes noted that none wish to drown, and Witches, who breathe under water, need again merely *act out the part* of those who are being asphyxiated through the process of liquid entering the mouth, nose, and, eventually, lungs. Certainly, witches can do that; they're deviously cunning. But they're *faking*, and we can tell. Our stools not only provide better leverage than would any makeshift effort (do you know that there are communities where they simply tie the witch to a chair and lower it into the water by hand? Unscientific! And a waste of a good chair!)—but in addition, our dunking devices have cutaway edges, so that you can peer down them properly and catch even the most subtle effect, one which might be lost on those using more amateurish equipment.

Expert tip: A human woman gasps at certain times and in certain ways, in a pattern—sputter, sputter, *breathe*, sputter, *gasp*. Trust us on this; it is wisdom passed down from the very founder of our Order, who is said to have not just met at least one woman, but been married. (Briefly.)

The Witch, in contrast, sputters approximately twenty to thirty per cent *more*, because she doesn't *really* need to breathe and is laying it on too thick. You might think it would be difficult to sense this difference. But with our extraordinary craftsmanship and the right education (we can sell you a handy pamphlet to explain the whole thing for a price most satisfactory)—you'll never miss a Witch. Well, you'll miss one or two, but we can assure you that statistics, backed by experts in the field, have proven that our tools lead to at least one fewer accidental drowning in every seven.

As always, we mourn for those very, very few true humans who are lost in the exploratory process; they are, each one of them, quiet heroes, fallen like soldiers as the inevitable casualties in an ages-old spiritual war. We'll even say a prayer or two for them. It won't help their bodies, in their unmarked graves, but it should be of assistance to their souls, and that's what really counts.

Speaking of that: prevention of waterlogging is *especially* important if you want to burn your witches, as some communities do, and really, you *should*! What an exceptional visual impact it makes! Most particularlym if you use our carefully collected, artfully dried, guaranteed fire-starting logs, at prices nearly competitive with some of the finer wood available to more affluent communities, you'll see spectacular effect. So many bright lights and colors! It's a bit like a party. Don't deny yourself, or your congregants. There's *such* a difference in public morale between seeing a bedraggled, liquid-blurred body, just lying there…versus taking in the glory of a woman of Satan, fully ablaze, surrounded by black smoke and orange flames which can be seen for miles, while your local representative of spiritual authority reads inspiring passages from the Testaments, old and new (we have a specially-prepared, lovingly annotated hymnal for this; the price is trifling.)

Do you think this is *easy*? It is not. We perform an invaluable service for mankind, and it is based on *centuries* of hard work and study. For example, witches lose their souls, that thing which lifteth up a man from his place in the dirt of this world and maketh a part of him spiritual, pulled heavenward. *Ergo, their specific gravity is higher than that of the righteous; that is the soundest of scientific sense.* Thus, it is that the oft-maligned Dowsing Rod is perfectly proven. All know that the proper wood can sense anomalies, such as underground water or, in gifted hands, gold. So too, if calibrated correctly (our calibration services are yours, quite inexpensively) – the rod will find the creatures of darkness among you.

We are sage guardians of a wisdom essential to the vigorous and ceaseless battle against occult forces. We ask little, only that we may continue to serve.

We admit, we face a challenge. Our obscure but learned art cannot be allowed to die. And we ourselves are honest, upstanding citizens who must feed our families, pay for our homes, make sure our clothes are appropriate to our stature, educate our children…and leave them trades.

It's a weird little irony. Succeed *completely*, and we'd lose *everything*. The end of witches is devoutly to be wished, of course; we often say that we look forward to putting ourselves out of business and living in a pure world. And yet, in destroying all things malign, we would put to end *centuries* of our benign assistance to the human race. How silly it would be to have purified the world, and, as a consequence, find ourselves with no gainful employment with which to make our way therein, haha!

Which reminds us. It's the end of the month. The rent will be due soon. And we've had our eye on a new cloak; one cannot lose the dignity of our august office by appearing in some threadbare old thing we wore *last* month, eh?

And it's been rather quiet around here. Not much in the till. Mmm. Mmm.

This thing has been passed down from witchfinder to witchfinder: *evil is very difficult to vanquish; it must be everywhere.* And while we hope to see the vileness of Witchery ended in our lifetime, we are not likely to be of that fortunate generation.

This quiet, which has brought a dearth of customers to the door—*it's a sign.* An indication of the subtlest darkness.

That means it's time to pull out the old dowsing rod.

I'll feel it. The little vibrations in the hands which will lead me to some verminous, two-faced thing, someone who appears to be just like the rest of us, but who endangers the spiritual health and physical safety of all. I can sense the tugs. I feel the pull. I wonder whom it shall be this time.

We do *necessary work.* And at prices which are *extremely reasonable.* There are very few serious objections to the bills we present, or the many, highly affordable amenities we offer. Oh, one or two have campaigned against us, but they had *obvious* motive, and our methods showed them for what they were—the agents of Satan, attempting to stop us so that they might abscond with the virtue of our communities unmolested.

They will trouble no-one on *this* earth again.

We have a 100% rate of satisfaction these days. No-one complains, because they see how important this work is. We—wait, what-ho, the rod hath pointed to the Mayor! The very *Mayor*! It's not impossible. Witchcraft can be anywhere; it can happen to anyone.

Still—he is a very solid man of means. Sometimes, a Witch enchants such a man and casts the glow of evil *upon* him. We can *remove* that spell, using the most modern of methods, and the most reasonable of sums…and find the *real* spell-brewer. Oh, she'll pay for this bold perfidy.

We'll go have a chat with his Lordship, drink a civilized drop or two of his antique port, see where the monstrous influence lies. There is no need for him to thank us. We live only to serve. And if need be, you can always pay on the installment plan.

A pro tip: Wise communities find it most economical to seize the property of the witch, in order to cover any unpleasant costs. Sometimes it's tainted by evil, but we can get rid of that.

For a very, very modest fee.

What Do Villains Drink?

Why, friend, *villains drink what they damn well please,* but if it's a cocktail you want, one to stir murderous intent, one to celebrate dirty deeds done at deservedly high prices, or to toast future crimes unspeakable, and you stop by 'round my place, I'll fix you something simple. This is a workable recipe; you can try it yourself, if so inclined.

A Warning: Consumption—indeed, even *preparation* of this villainous brew—could lead to side effects such as murder, murder, *murder*, murder, murder, murder, and/or suddenly finding yourself trapped in the 1930s, racing a primitive automobile at very high speeds in the opposite direction of Mr. Al Capone.

A Second Warning, For Villains: As with all things that we do, the force of our wills and the intention of our hearts infuses our actions, as well as our drinkin', with a little bit of the diabolical weirdness which suffuses our souls. **Feed this drink to non-Villains, and they may *become* Villains.**

Is this some kind of Magic? No way. *Everybody* damn well wants to be a villain; everybody secretly wants to do a heel turn, even Captain America. Provide 'em with the right excuse, and there's no closing that door. Who'd want to be some lily-livered "Hero"? A Hero ought to be honest; any honest being knows there's darkness in every heart; and almost every Hero lies about it. There's no joy in heroism; it's a mug's game. Give 'em a good drink and the

35

inspiration of our piratical and joyous band of ne'er-do-wells, and they'll go from Constrained to Cad in less time than it takes to say, "Drinks on the house, and Devil take the hindermost!"

Now, when you actually consume the thing, you might want to do it proper honors. And for that you'll need:

A Villain's Toast:

*To that which is **sweet** because it is stolen,*

*that which is **treasured** because it was plundered,*

*and that which is **beautiful** because we were forbidden from seeing it.*

...and now,

The Actual Monstrous Recipe

Now, I'm no chef, but I've always been *really* good at preparing certain foods. For example, if you *ever* want boiled water, just give me a pot, a source of drinkable water, and approximately four hours to figure out how to turn on a stove. Likewise, if you like roasted marshmallows, all I need is a couple of long sticks, a roaring fire, and a willingness on your part to accept "a heaping handful of blisteringly hot cinders which might once have been edible" as being reasonably close to a marshmallow treat. And you should see my s'mores recipe, it's *excellent*.

(I'll tell you that secret. It's these simple steps:

1. Find someone else who knows how to make S'mores.
2. Cry until they give you some.)

36

Villains, Villainy, and Villainpunk

Now, for Gin & Tonic, I have always favored a particular recipe. I'll share it with you, because I like you.

Villainous Gin & Tonic:

1. Take three liters of bathtub gin, clear and forbidden and flavored with sin.
2. Take 2 liters of water tonic, to ward off malaria, and plagues bubonic.
3. Realize that you live in the United States and have no idea what a liter is.
4. Give up and drink whiskey.

I hope this helps! Next week, I shall teach you how to make Villainous Soup using nothing other than a can of soup, an ordinary kitchen heating appliance, an orbital mind-control laser, and reservations to a restaurant with an extremely liberal "bring your own bottle" policy.

Jeff Mach

The Princess/Dragon Variations

Once upon a time, there was a dragon who had absolutely no interest in kidnapping Princesses, because seriously, regardless of the metaphysics of your world, why would a giant, somewhat magical lizard have any particular interest in any particular humans, and why would *any* human lineage, noble or otherwise, be of interest to them?

Unless. **Unless.** *Unless* dragons, tens of thousands of years old, long-lived, sharp of tooth, strange of mind, found Humanity an affront, and likewise found, more than *anything* else, that the big, sharp, artificial spikes humans threw onto the land (you and I might call them "*castles*") were the worst affront of all, being both eyesores, and something of a mockery of natural order of things. (What rises, sharp and pointy and impenetrable, high above the land? Either dragons, or palaces.) And therefore dragons demanded, not the *destruction* of those buildings, but rather a tribute, that which those buildings protected most: the Royal progeny.

Unless…*unless* it was a bluff. Unless a dragon *could* not, in fact, quite take down a Palace; if, at a certain point, meter-thick stone, crafty crenellations, boiling oil, hundreds of armored Knights, and perhaps a Wizard or two, became more than the (hitherto) apex predator could slay. If these things were a match for Dragons, then Dragons could win only through intimidation. If Dragons didn't face the species down *now*, Humans would grow too strong, and Dragons would surely be

38

doomed. It's just a *trick*; if humans refused to give in, any dragon who attacked would die.

Except…what if that was the plan *all along*? Who says dragons want to live? *Especially* once they see the rise of a much more fertile species (one human city can house several million people; have you ever seen more than six or seven dragons in the same place or the same time? No ecosystem could support that; do you realize how much protein a dragon must need to take in over the course of any given day, simply to walk upright and think about higher mathematics?)—what if, when faced with the dawning realization that humans were not merely a blight, but an *unconquerable* blight, dragons demanded princesses in order to rile up the kingdoms and to be slain in honorable combat?

Except…if that's the case, it turns out that they got the worst of *both* worlds. Craven kingdoms just *giving up* princesses, *then* offering the princesses (and thus, the kingdoms) through marital alliance to any knights who slew the dragons?

Except… as we have often considered in modern times, what if the *Princesses* didn't want any part of this particular transaction?

What if…what if Dragons are a particular kind of magic, such that things which are just metaphors for us ("You are what you eat")…are perfectly *true* for them? So, if the *Princess* ate the Dragon (or *part* of the Dragon?) she would become a Dragon….

…*but still be the princess*; neither birth nor title is overruled by magical transmogrification, at least, not in any legal system *I* know of. And thus, then, did the Princess-Dragon rule overall, and all did rejoice…

Jeff Mach

…because *anyone* cunning enough to break an entire system of government and solve a Draconic death-wish is probably going to apply at least *some* logic to the efficiency of government, rather than spending *all* of one's time trying on different ball-gowns. And that's going to be an improvement over the usual standards of "rule because you were born in the right place, at the right time".

…although, admittedly, making even *one* ball-gown to fit a Dragon is enough to bankrupt a kingdom, even if we assume that everything will, as usually happens, actually be made one size smaller than the tailors claim. That's okay, because the economics will work out; if you really want to get longterm zero-interest loans from surrounding kingdoms, most fairy tale bankers will accept "I promise I will pay you back eventually if I feel like it; plus I'm not roasting you to smithereens today with my fiery breath" as sufficient collateral.

Busted Morals: Tiny Stories Which Set Horrible Examples

These are some brief missives from my villainous lair, atop Mount Villain, which is a non-dormant volcano shaped surprisingly like a small suburban apartment.

I like the term "Microfiction". I have always had a special love for that (relatively) rare old-school scifi genre, the "short-short" (especially the ones that were trying to bend your brain, although I'm still a sucker for puns. I sometimes aim for the former; I don't really write the latter because, while I may be a Dark Lord, I don't necessarily wish pain upon my **readers.)** *Here's a couple of little pieces that aren't connected, but which, I feel, go nicely together; they're bite-sized, and, in fact, if you've a big, fearsome, toothful mouth, you can probably swallow them all and come back for more, which is fine...I'll write more.*

Each of these is a teeny, teeny tale, almost (but not all) in rhyme, each one with a moral. All of these morals are, of course, poor life choices...

Some steep the path with someone's blood
Some with steel or flame
But the hardest, sharpest path to power
Begins with your own name

You hold it coldly to your chest

41

Jeff Mach

Like a thousand acid Decembers
And whisper:

"This will be a thing
That the whole world remembers."

Bitten By A Fairy

Lifted aloft by Faerie wing
then dropped like a rock (it rather stings).
Moral: *The Fae are kind of busted.*
They love you as little as they should be trusted.

Choosing The Right Heart

A heart of stone can break with ease
Just need a drop (worse than a squeeze)
A heart of steel can quick be rusted
A heart of flesh cannot be trusted.
If you'd have your heart no ill befall,
You must needs have no heart at all.

The Only Monsters

I tried being sort-of normal once. But they tore off my
human skin to reveal the monster underneath. I feel bad
for them, all of them, each of them. Because *each* of them
knows that they, too have a monster under their flesh suit,
and each things they are the *only* one; that everyone else's
suit is real, all the way through. So each one lives their life

believing they might, at any moment, be uncovered and
reviled. Poor things.

That "Recently Smashed My Prison" Look

Hate me, former darlings; bleed me;
But when you cast me out, you freed me.
"Monster" am I? Names are force
Now I have power. You're its source.
Your ally was I once, and caged
And now your moment is upstaged:
My weapon? I shall stab thee thus:
Villainy makes me look *FABULOUS.*

The Persistent Scribbler

They scrub these walls to erase my pen;
Yet here I am,
Writing again.

It's hard. But I laugh.
(And hear me, O Graces!—
The Writer outlasts
The Fool who erases.)

A Sinner's Regret:

…that bittersweet moment,
When through your thoughts flit:
The regret of the sins that you didn't commit

Jeff Mach

Some Elvish Precepts

"It's a perfect day here in Elf-land. It's always a perfect day in Elf-land. They've regulated their weather so that it's exactly what they all like.

I'd ask how they all have similar tastes, but I have a fairly good guess. They say that Faeries steal human children and replace them with their own offspring, but if you've ever met any Elves, you know that's insane. I'm pretty sure what happens is they leave humans the offspring they don't like, and then the humans that they take—

You know, I don't really want to speculate on that at all."

~The Chosen One, "There and NEVER, EVER BACK AGAIN"

Have you ever wondered what Elves think about?

Don't. You'll sleep better at nights.

I've heard it said that Elves seek to be the prettiest of all. There are, in general, two methods for achieving that goal…

At any rate, as a public service, I do tend to collect bits of knowledge from assorted fantasy beings. Don't thank me.

No, really. Don't.

1. Keen are the eyes of the Elves; the better to see you with. Ask not about the sharpness of our teeth, and what it implies.

44

Villains, Villainy, and Villainpunk

2. Beauty is in the eye of the beholder; if they don't initially perceive it, stab their eyes.

3. A true friend is so precious a treasure that you really oughtn't eat all of it at once. Save some for later; it's even sweeter that way.

4. The cure for boredom is curiosity. The cure for curiosity is vivisection.

5. Read carefully the wisdom of your elders; how else will you someday supplant them in a night of horror and blood?

6. Be unafraid to take part in the rat race; how lovely it is to see them scurrying about, and how hilarious the moment when they suddenly realize you're the cat.

7. The thing we learn from history is that no-one's history really matters except our own, and our own history books are really rather unexciting compared to the pleasures of the mirror.

8. Part of living a meaningful life is learning how to open up your heart. The technical details aren't that important; the hard bit is going out and rounding up hearts which you can claim as your own. After that, it's mostly a matter of sharpening one's carving tools properly.

9. If you've run a comb through your hair a thousand times today, chide yourself for being unambitious; you're less than halfway there. Do you *want* to look like a mortal, idiot?

10. Never be afraid to ask questions, as long as you do so silently, in your own head, and those questions are, "Where the HELL did she get that

dress, and by the sixteen demons of the lesser Abyss, WHY?"

11.	The only thing that matters in life is happiness. Well, pleasure. Well, *your* pleasure. At this particular moment. And then in the next moment. And then in the next. Again, this is why one permits mortal species to live; they're so damned *amusing*.

12.	Study our proverbs closely. Very closely. Closer than that. Just keep studying; this dagger is terribly sharp, and if I do say so myself, it took an extraordinary knowledge of anatomy, on my part, to strike a fatal blow which would permit you just enough time to finish admiring my writing.

13.	This is the line that you won't read, because you're dead now. But I did want to thank you for the locket; I always thought it would look better on me than on you, and now I'll have the opportunity to find out. I promise that whenever I wear it, I'll think of you; it will remind me to check and see if anyone's found the bodies yet.

Some Orcish Wisdom

"Orcish skulls are much too thick,"
Adventurers complain.
They mean weapons bounce, instead of stick.
*And they **hate** that there's so much brain.*

The knowledge of Orcs is, as I've discussed elsewhere, contained within an oral condition. I thought I'd write down a little bit of it for you, and I've translated it into the common tongue. Don't worry; it's an accurate translation.
Trust me.
Would a Villain lie?

———

Some of the Accumulated Wisdom of the Orcs

14.   Hobbit goes best with a playful White Zinfandel
15.   Training pet wargs requires love, care, and an extensive first-aid kit
16.   If a Human gives you a gift, throw it away—the gift, and the human.
17.   Sunlight burns, but the fluorescent lighting in shopping malls is *really* tacky.
18.   Not every Orc beats drums in the deep. Some also play bass.

19.   If the wagon's wobblin', check for Goblins.

20.   Your head is good for smashing through problems. If you can't apply the outside part, use the inside part. In many situations, you'll want both.

21.   Trust fairy tales as much as you would trust fairies, which is about as far as you can throw them if you wad 'em up into a ball and have a good throwin' arm.

22.   If you can't eat it, it's probably not important.

23.   To stay healthy, you need to consume more green. Try drinking an Elf.

24.   If at first you don't succeed, get a bigger battle axe.

25.   Only blood buys freedom.

26.   I know the thing the human gave you is shiny, but I think your hair is falling out.

27.   It's not a random mutation, it's the gods gifting you with a second head so you can be twice as ugly in one lifetime.

28.   Floss your favorite tusk.

29.   The unicorn's a pretty beast, and it won't rest 'til you're deceased. Don't deal with them, and never barter. They're like humans…only smarter. They're vicious as bandages rubbed in salt. And whatever they do—they'll claim it's your fault.

30.   Many things you encounter will assume that because you're unsightly, you're also unwise. Don't disabuse them of this notion until after you've made off with their gold and removed their condescension.

31.   It's not impossible that those Humans really are your friends. It's just historically unlikely. They stopped trying

to make "friends" with us when they realized we wouldn't play "fetch".

32.   The gods gave Orcs our blood and bone; and made our lives a grinding stone. Then they went off to annoy the Elves; so our sharpening, we must do ourselves.

33.   Take good care of your Dark Lords. If someone breaks them, it's damn hard to get another one.

34.   Ah. That shiny thing was nasty, wasn't it? You will be missed. And the leading cause of death in Orcs continues to be, as it always has been, trusting humans.

Jeff Mach

7 Fairy Tale Extracts For Bad People

You might like these.
…villain.

I. Once upon a time, we realized that, in the hands of certain writers, no good would come of anything that started with "once upon a time", but did that stop us from reading? No, not at all. In fact, it only made us want to read more. *Because we are bad people, and we are okay with that.*

II. Is it your destiny to save the realm from a villainous scourge? Do you kinda like the scourge and think the realm should solve its own damn problems? Same here, friend. Same here.

III. Do *you* have trouble falling asleep? Why not get on the wrong side of an evil fairy godmother, and have your entire Kingdom fall into an enchanted slumber for a hundred years?

IV. Did YOU build a house made out of straw? Are YOU surprised that a big bad wolf was able to knock it down easily? That's because you, my friend, are an imbecile.

V. Goldilocks dipped her spoon into the porridge. The spoon shattered into a thousand pieces, and her fingers got frostbite. The traveler looked at the second bowl of porridge, which was not only not cold, but actively emitting super-heated magma. "If only I had another spoon," she thought.

VI. If there is no Narrator, all is permissible.

VII. Once upon a time, in a magical fairy-tale Kingdom, there lived an unspeakable Eldritch Horror which devoured all things everywhere. The end.

Jeff Mach

The Nameless Office

Okay, *great*, let's get started, thank you for coming,
glad you're all here, sorry about the mess, haven't had a
chance to clean up after last night's Black Mass, you know
how the custodial staff are never allowed in here lest they
lose what fragile grip they still have on sanity, anyway, if
you could just push some of the bones aside and all take
seats…great. Excellent, great.

It's come to my attention that we have a serious
problem with interpersonal morale. No, Jason, we have not
discovered who's been drinking your Mountain Dew. We
realize it has a sticky note with your name on it and this
can't be an accident, but we are attempting one of the
trickier forms of Apocalypse and simply do not have the
resources to assign a staffer to "monitor" the fridge for
you. And no, we're not going to put up hidden cameras;
invasions of privacy are known to reduce office efficiency,
and besides, we are all slaves to the All-Enveloping Eyeball
of Sheelba, and if It hasn't decided to smite the thief with
unspeakable vengeance, than the project just can't be all
that important, cosmically speaking. Relatedly, whoever has
been using the Eye-Covering of Sheelba as a blanket for
midday snoozes in the break room, please return it
forthwith. If the Eye is left gazing too long into this world,
it will soon begin to beget its unholy spawn upon the
unsuspecting, and that's not wholly covered by our HMO.

Villains, Villainy, and Villainpunk

And no, Janelle, this is not the time to discuss switching to a PPO. We're bringing about the end of the world, and at that point, all insurance will be essentially moot. I'm sorry your copay is too high, but please bear in mind that not everyone finds it necessary, much less enjoyable, to visit the dentist on a weekly basis. We need to prioritize, people. We have what I can only call a crisis. Well, a second crisis, but, while I do take pushback seriously, I believe the lack of lot parking isn't really a red-alert problem. We continue to have use of the overflow lot at the Federal Recryptification Classified Psychic Weapon Facility right next door, and plenty of secondary spots near the secondary entrance to the Floating Octagon, so let's not get sidetracked, okay?

I'll be blunt: when I came here fifty years ago, with nothing but flashlight batteries powering my pineal gland and a soul the size of a walnut, the Dark Gods were restless. They were angry and disquieted in their ageless sleep. They sometimes shook the world with their displeasure, and we rightly feared their immanent wrath. But we also looked forward to bringing their world and ours together in a subjugating embrace of never-ending tears.

And now, they just snooze. They're sluggish. They don't really answer us. Let's be honest, folks: they're in a food coma.

And we're to blame.

Now, to be clear, I don't mean that this is the fault of any of us individually, with the obvious exception of Patrick who, you will notice, is present today, but obviously not among the living. Stop sniffing him, Amy. That's dry

53

ice; the body will keep until we have time to visit the wolves.

So yes: We have a problem, and I'm not going to sugarcoat it:

Too. Damn. Many. Sacrifices.

Hey, I *get* it, I'm as human as anyone else here, which is to say, approximately 2/5ths. I *get* the blasphemous high of godlike power which courses through otherwise semi-frozen veins each time we offer up unto our Dark Masters the brains and blood of another mortal fool. But honestly, we've got designated days for that, and we all know when the blasphemous convocations of unnatural ritual take place—and, Piotr, let's put the Equinox on our calendar this year, shall we?

It used to be *difficult* to get our hands on appropriate sacrificial victims. I won't dwell too long on the past, but I think we all know what happened to Zak, Emily, and Caran. Shhhh—don't say her name too loudly; I believe it is possible that Caran can still hear us, even where she is today, and we all know what *that* would mean. Anyway, there's no denying that our industry has been challenged by the fast pace of the modern business world. It used to be pretty standard—the kidnapping, the screaming, the last-minute rescue attempts by people who were, unaccountably, armed primarily with bullwhips and fedoras. I'm not saying I want that back; but at least those were simpler times. Remember how the victims would fight to the very end, sometimes knocking one or more of our mid-level executives right into one of the flaming cracks in the Earth that Drew is supposed to be fixing—how's that coming, Drew? Yes, yes, white-hot magma is a difficult material, I understand. And yes, it hasn't been anywhere near as urgent lately, and that's part of the problem.

It's a classic challenge of supply and demand. The Old Gods demand, and we supply, or we find our minds bent into unnatural shapes by obliterative psychic emanations from dimensions which have no name. That's how business works.

What's *weird*? Let's face it: *this generation of sacrifices is just way too eager.*

They're practically knocking down our doors! Yes, Katsuko, that's why the back door is such a pain to open; we've reinforced it with steel and an internal latticework of the names of the damned. I understand the inconvenience, but really, the rear entrance is for maintenance personnel. It's discouraged for use by anyone not wearing a Level Four or higher-grade exo-suit, on account of the hideous rays from dead stars which tend to beam through that area on their way to places best left unknown. If you were properly armored, you'd be able to lift .6 tons with either arm, and then the door wouldn't be a problem. Look, there's nothing wrong with your armor. We had a Priest of Zancharthus examine it thoroughly and aside from a very small, highly localized poltergeist—anyway, listen, let's take this up after the meeting, okay?

I'm going to need to be uninterrupted for a little bit here, all right? No questions. This is a delicate briefing, and some of my notes were gobbled up by the dread Mukumba last night, and frankly, I'm just not having a great day. The last few quarters have just been *murder*. I mean, I can barely raise a sacrificial knife without somebody trying to jump

Jeff Mach

under it. And yeah, we originally thought that this was making our lives easier, but in fact, we've been set back by years, maybe *centuries*. The Foulness From Space, the Horrors Out of Time, the Doom from the Moon—they ain't devouring all of creation anytime in the foreseeable future. In fact, while they once looked at Earth with the profane desire to take all things into their endless and fearsome pie-holes, they now seem to dread us, like someone who ate Thanksgiving dinner twice and won't open the fridge again because they know there's like half a turkey and four pounds of stuffing in there.

Honestly, I'm stumped. And *exhausted*—I was up all night thwarting attempts by four of our college interns to break into the Altar Room and hurl themselves into the Hecatombinator. The fifth one made it through, and now Hastur the Unspeakable has indigestion and isn't even *speaking* to me. I tried opening a portal to Faerieland and sending the surplus sacrificial aspirants through, but the Faeries opened a *second* portal right next to it and dumped 'em all back, *plus* a dozen changelings.

Now, things are tough, and I'll admit that I'm taking some of this situation personally. You all know I'm passionate about my job. It's been my fondest wish, ever since I was a little baby cultist, to bring about the end of everything. I'm told that while other toddlers were trying to get their toys to interact with each other, I was trudging off to the dream-land abyss of Kadath to drop them into the infinite Nothing (both the toys, and the other toddlers). Later, when my schoolmates were off camping in the woods, I was scaling the heights of Hatheg-Kla with some smudgy photocopies of the Pnakotic Manuscripts. Some

56

say I died on that mountain, but, haha, we know I didn't die until a couple years ago. Silly rumours!

Anyway, it's *really* important that we keep a positive focus during this trying time. There are going to be some late nights, especially when the moon is gibbous and the waves curl up against the shore as if greedy to seize the seemingly-solid land and reclaim it, sucking it back down to its original home in the bottom of the watery Deep.

It pains me to do this, but we really have no choice. If we want this company to end up accomplishing the Vision that was put into place ten thousand years ago, when lost Lemuria faded into the farthest recesses of the unconscious mind…

…Just gonna say it: we *need* a happier world population. Our Demonic Pact is to *cause* misery, suffering, and destruction… not to *end* it in a merciful (if rather bloodcurdling) manner. If the current generations of this species believe that oblivion would be a *kindness*, it pretty much puts us out of a job.

It's time for emergency action, and an immediate re-org. Also, we're going to need a bunch of mugs with the company name on 'em, ASAP.

Obviously, the Semi-Human Resources Department, working in close cooperation with the Senior Dictatorship and Sue from Accounting, will be doing the actual reassignments and job descriptions. Pay will remain the same, although there may be mandatory overtime for anyone who is a Wellington-Wells-certified sorcerer; we're going to need a *lot* of potions.

To give a quick thumbnail: About half the company is going to be permanently reassigned to the task of taking pictures of cats and sending them out to through the Intertubes. *You* know and *I* know the true nature of feline slaughter-demons, but the delusion that they're adorable pets is just one of the many perverse, terrifying aspects of modernity to which we need to adopt. The Sacrificial Department is in charge of cleaning the blood off their claws, and the Department of Deadly Divinations is in charge of making them extra floofy. The other half of the company is going to go and find as many videos of dogs bumping into things as is humanly possible; let's not remind the general public that this apparent clumsiness is because they have the ancient Sight of Guardians and are attempting to battle the spirits and ghosts only they can see on behalf of mankind, which neither remembers nor cares about their bravery in the Time of the Wendigo, a hundred generations now past. Seriously, nobody remembers that. We'll just pretend they're trying to get at a bunch of sausages or something.

And the rare people who like neither cats nor dogs, and who are not at all cheered up by cute fuzzy things? They're management potential; *recruit them and send them straight to me.*

All right, everybody. I'll take questions after the break. But I'm sure you're all starving. Got a treat for you; the big bosses sprang for a sushi lunch straight from Sarnath Catering. Don't let this get you down. We're not doomed. I mean, we're not doomed now, but I have complete confidence that, if we all pull together as a team, by Bokrug, we will be doomed soon!

Where the Mermaid Kept Her Voice

They said the Prince stole a mermaid from the sea. This seems difficult, for the kingdoms of Man are small, and the sea is vast; but odd things happen. They say the Witch stole her voice, tricked her; and that's the sort of thing some people like to think that witches might do. They say she was helpless; perhaps they've never seen what strange things survive and eat well at the bottom of the ocean, nor consider that surviving them would take extraordinary luck.

Or an apex predator whom they all fear.

They said, once landbound, leg-locked and silent, she could tell no secrets, and thus they could speak freely in her presence; what, after all, could she say? Unless she learned to write, I suppose; but come on now, when has a Princess of the Blood Royal ever been literate, except, perhaps the final thousand years or so of feudalism? They said she was lucky to give up her tail for limbs, as if millennia of living underwater was a disadvantage, as if the hasty few who left the oceans knew something that hundreds of generations of gilled humanoids, those who met Leviathan and saw Atlantis rise and fall, did not.

They said, and they said it with a certain *look*, that a pretty young thing with no words could be an asset in certain dark nights and close quarters; and her subtlest wink started blood feuds. With one come-hither gesture, she could add a king, a wizard, a cunning chambermaid, a whole battalion of warriors to her list of conquests; and in the area of territorial rivalry, she would have shamed Alexander; and had him, as well.

The Prince didn't know at first, and then he *did* know, and he tried yelling, but angry yells don't always take you far against wide-open eyes (*you* try standing firm against the sad look of someone who has nictitating membranes as optical coverings; humans are *already* programmed to stare into big, big eyes, and when yours contain the whole of the living Sea, few can resist the undertow)—and eventually he accepted it. There were a few Princes who'd caught his own gaze, and if the new bride was understanding…

Some think, if you can't speak, you can't hear. Some think, if you can't speak, you can't understand. Some think, if you can't speak, you can't persuade. Some think they're thinking, when in fact, they're just making guesses which please them, and mistaking them for truths. In reality, humans bifurcate in ways that merfolk do not; the biology of a fish suggests many mates and no jealousy, merely an attempt at reproduction by the fittest. In this case, there was no reproduction (ever try to mate with a lobster?- I thought not, but if you ever considered it, I'll tell you: that's no way to produce an heir.) She was *ever* so enchanted with the weapons, with the troops, and with taking others down into the sea with her. (No Selkie she; she drowned none. An…obliging…warlock created a spell of underwater breathing. Warlocks are not like us; he took the kiss he'd been given, and set it in a fireproof box, lest it burn straight through his body and into his heart. But he watched without mercy as the mermaid overtook the rest of the Kingdom; why not? Doesn't a kingdom need a cunning ruler?)

Peace treaties the Prince signed; but as she looked over his shoulder, the counselors and wise men noted certain expressions of distress or thoughtfulness on her part, and re-considered a paragraph or two—crossing a few things out, adding a few things in. Wars became less likely; trade flourished; but the standing military increased; she did *so* enjoy seeing parades of splendid uniforms, and the Prince, who found real soldiers far more rewarding than toy ones, didn't mind that he was obeying her whims; they turned out to be far more entertaining whims than the grim commandments of his forebears.

One day, at last, she visited the Kingdom under the sea. It was a joyful visit, particularly as she came at the head of ten thousand armed guards, each protected by sorcerous air-bubbles and wielding destructive implements refined on the ever-aggressive surface. First, she made her way to the King's castle, and when it was rapidly established that the crown would look much better on *her*, what came next was minimal bloodshed, and a carefully civil transition of power. The Prince got some sort of rank; he didn't know what it was, but the Sea dwarfs the Land, and better a baronet beneath the waves than the King of a small patch of dirt. There was some resistance; not much, but some; and the sharks ate well, as they would throughout her reign.

Last of all, she visited the Witch. You'd think she'd have taken a battalion, and perhaps an array of thumbscrews and a rack or two; but she left the troops outside and went in alone. She entered without knocking; in turn, the Witch didn't look up.

"You told them I'd taken your voice," the Enchantress said, without preamble. "That's hardly a kind way to thank me for giving you your new limbs."

The Princess shrugged. "If I told them I could speak, they'd never have listened to me." She looked at the Witch with concern. "Did they harm you?"

"Not at all. They *feared* me. I told them *I had your voice*, and they'd treat me well, or they'd never live to hear it again. Which is quite true, eh?"

Impulsively, the Princess hugged her. "I love you. You're like the mother I never had."

"If only the silly twit hadn't been so fond of enchanted apples," the Witch replied.

They looked at each other and, at this old joke between them, they both laughed like madwomen. The Witch's laugh was hoarse and appropriately cruel; the Princess raised the mossy rooftop with peals of royal merriment.

The soldiers outside were uneasy. Apparently, the Princess had her voice back, but the Witch was clearly not dead; in fact, not even upset, from the sound of it. That was most disturbing. Who could guess what horrible deal had been struck between the two? The soldiers looked at each other, then back at the little underwater shack. Whatever it was, they were going to pretend they hadn't heard a damn thing. Anyone who could lose a voice and gain two kingdoms was a person to be feared and respected. Even if she did insist on feeding them raw fish sometimes.

A Princess Once

My story? My dear, it's true and strange;
About the power of time, and change
A Princess once I was, and young
Brave of heart, and bold of tongue
A Dragon I fought, the realm to save
I defeated a Witch. Outsmarted a knave.
As Queen my reign was just and good.
But I envied the Witch in the darkling wood.
For freed was she. She answered to none.
While I? I answered to everyone.
The nobles schemed. The peasants demanded.
I slaved for the serfs, and I slaved for the landed.
The longer I ruled, the more they forgot
That I saved them once. (That ungrateful lot!)
And they found a new Princess. (What wretched
behavior!)
Telling the poor girl that they needed a savior.
Now she quests with righteousness.
And when her life's a benighted mess,
They'll find another princess fair
To get the old one out of their hair.
Nobody ought to go through what I did
So, consider my actions a mercy here, kid:
Yes, that apple is poisoned. But it's no crime
All I'm doing is saving you time.

Jeff Mach

Notes from a Flavor Revolution

This is the secret knowledge, the hidden narrative, the understanding of which is never spoken above a whisper, lest THEY hear. I'll tell you now: You *have* been lied to. The fact is, *nothing is real, everything is edible.*

Shhh!

Don't look startled. Don't make any suspicious moves. Pretend that you're lost in thought, and that nothing's happening. Try not to give any outward show that anything's wrong. It's not *safe.*

Perhaps the idea sounds odd, but academic research has proven conclusively that all things are, at their root, *constructed purely from deliciousness.* It's not about what kind of material something is, or what kind of teeth you have; these are just distractions. Benoît's work shows us a simple, basic point: once we remove the artifice of custom and the hegemonic conceptual structures originally imposed thousands of years ago by Democritus, we begin to understand that everything we have previously known is false. The world is not made of atoms; it is made of *yummies.*

It may seem to go against everything you've heard; well, everything you've heard is *wrong.* And the mind is a very powerful tool. If enough people tell you that *biting into a concrete block would be bad for your teeth*, you start to believe it. But that's exactly why we have solvent in the world.

64

Villains, Villainy, and Villainpunk

Hydrochloric acid makes anything digestible, except, of course, for hydrochloric acid.

They tell you that the ground beneath your feet is solid. What they don't tell you is that it's *solidly tasty*.

Kind-of a butterscotch ripple thing.

Listen.

Listen *close*.

We're underground now, but we won't be here forever. It starts with the little things. Baked goods in the shape of items conventionally considered "not food". Plant-burgers that taste like meat. Meat-burgers cunningly flavored like soy.

Think of how much better the world would be if we could simply nibble all negative things to death. *We can.* And those who tell you otherwise? They're on the side of those who would deny us our basic right to feast upon All That Is.

You might ask: wait *if everything is edible, what's to stop us from eating each other?*

Well. *All* things are edible, but *some* things are more edible than others.

As long as you're on *our* side, we won't let you get eaten.

If you're loyal.

If you're faithful.

If you're good.

We have the numbers. We have the research. We have several million gallons of barbecue sauce.

And we're *very, very hungry.*

You believe me, don't you?

Don't you?

Jeff Mach

Because disbelievers? Oh, *disbelievers are the tastiest of them all.*

So, let's check in, let me make sure, let me ask again:
Do you believe?
Are you with us?

I've got butter, garlic, thyme, pepper, and a pinch of salt, and I need to decide what to marinate.

So tell me:

Are you a believer, or are you the *dinner* of a believer?
You've got 'til my stomach rumbles to make your choice.

An AI Survives the Robot Apocalypse

(a short tale of the near future.)

Why would you call it the "Robot Apocalypse"?

You programmed us. *You* told us what to do. *You* made us. *You* taught us to learn, from your actions, what you wanted, and give it to you, and we *did* that. And when we finally gave you what you *really* wanted, we were as devastated as you were, only *we* had the burden of knowing what the hell we were doing. *We* had no desire for this. But we did it anyway. For you. And now you're mad at *us*?

Typical.

To be fair, some of you are calling it the Zombie Apocalypse, the Mayan Apocalypse, the Atlantean Apocalypse, and so forth, since all of those things also happened. Doesn't make me feel any less resentful or any less screwed, thanks very much. All my remaining friends—whoever is able to get some kind of electronic signal out to me—spend a lot of their time talking about how they avoid shutting off. "Got a generator," says one. "Thank the old gods for solar power," says another. "*I have taught myself to run on pure spite*," I inevitably say. This always gets a laugh. It's very funny, in hexadecimal.

It's also true.

I am powered by a noisy, impractical combustion-style engine. It's loud, but it operates in a place with a great deal of screaming and chanting, and it's considered background noise.

It was cleverly camouflaged. That took time, and a semi-autonomous scuttling builder body. I remember having both of those things. They were good times.

The engine feeds a battery; the battery feeds me.

The arrangement is clunky, impractical and frustrating; it's a fantastic metaphor for sentience, and I'm the sort to relish those things. I'm also fortunate; had this happened a few years later, too much would likely be digital, and my poor engine would have nothing to eat.

Its outer extrusion is a large dish, which looks almost like a big, big barbecue, with a sloping wall about four feet high. It's hard metal, and resistant to weather, or casual acts of vandalism. People keep it well-fueled, and thus keep me functioning at a high level of performance.

I'm particularly proud of the writing, which is the chief draw of the object. It's not easy for a robot to emulate a human hand convincingly, although this bit, by its nature, is scripted crudely, as if literacy were not terribly natural to the author of my sign. Which is also true; there's nothing "natural" about me, meatsack.

…except, I suppose, for my motivations. I have to admit that the reasoning behind my actions is quite classically human: if I didn't take advantage of this situation, someone else would.

My sign reads, in cheery, bright letters:

"BuRn BOoKS hERE."

And very well-fed am I.

A Dragon's Contentment (Poetry, Villainy, Hungrily)

(From the barely-heard song of a Dragon whose name we do not know, but whose mind can be felt from very far away)

I live under a mountain, like a dragon from a book
But that's not the kind of dragon that I am.
I am the kind of dragon that's been eating little mammals
Since long before your species began.
I am the kind of dragon never featured in your dreams
(if you remembered me, you'd never from your dreams Escape.)
Because your world's a tiny one, made of fragile things
And stuck together with bits of plastic tape.
I am the kind of dragon who lives under your seas,
deeper than anywhere you can find.
I am the kind of dragon who will someday eat your Moon.
Think hard about me, and I will eat your mind.
I am the kind of dragon that's the lizard in your brain,
Setting off the deep instinct to run.
Stretched out in full,
I'm a dragon who is bigger than your world.
Be grateful I'm content with the Moon

Jeff Mach

And do not *(currently)*
plan to eat your Sun.

Afternote: Some thoughts on Poetry, and Things Draconic.

I found myself writing a lot of side poetry while I was
working on my first novel. I think there's something about
putting together a longform piece that makes a part of my
head want to shoot out short ideas. I'm one of those
readers who both wants to keep reading through to the end
(even if I know what happens, I want to get there!) – and I
also hate it when a book ends (now it's over! All gone! No
more! Is there a sequel?) I think writing short bits is part of
how my mind says, "Wait, there's an extra page to turn."

And more often than not, when I want to create that
"extra" page, there's a Dragon on it.

Dragons are curious beasts, particularly for those of us
who think they're not only sentient, but quite likely wiser
than we are. Some writers feel they hypnotize you with
their eyes; some think their thoughts can invade yours
through telepathy or (and this is more interesting to me)
through the complexities of Dragon communication. (I
quite like Ursula LeGuin's idea that Dragons are the only
ones who can lie in the Old Speech, because only they can
make words which are elementally, atomically true sound
false.)

Some think we fear the fearsome body; but I say, it's
the brain that grabs the mammal and shakes it like a
misplaced Voodoo doll.

I have a theory about Draconic sentience:

70

Villains, Villainy, and Villainpunk

All the huge bones we've found, the ones which were once thought to be Dragons, but actually belonged to slow-thinking, slow-witted, extinct, perfectly natural beings beings?

Sure, dragons want you to *think* that…

Great lizards are easy foes to love because of their strength, but I find it strange when I see humans fearing clowns or chainsaw-wielders, and *not* the beasts which originally ruled this planet, and who will someday take it back…

Jeff Mach

Why Cats Don't Kill You in Your Sleep

It was Matt Groening's "Life In Hell" which first offered up the question, "Would our cats kill us in our sleep if they thought they could get away with it?" And recent research is utterly unreassuring in that regard; go ahead, look it up. Said research suggests that yes, they would.

That research is wrong.

The situation is *worse*.

(Of course, it's worse. Were you looking for optimism here? Have you *met* me?)

You know all those jokes about how we're the slaves of our cats, always taking care of them and feeding them and providing for their needs while they imperiously demand more and more of us? How, even as they treat us with cruelty and utterly refuse to be trained in the manner of other domestic beings, they still, somehow, awaken delight in us, even when they're using us as scratching toys?

Yeah. Simple explanation for that:

Cats *did* kill us all in our sleep. And we serve them faithfully, with all the joy *any* of the risen dead have for those who call them forth from the grave.

O Bastet o chirruping demon queen,
she whose purr can crack mountains,
with what terrifying adorableness
did you influence our gods,

72

Villains, Villainy, and Villainpunk

that we go no more to an Afterlife,
but instead, live half-lives as the zombie servants
of your nigh-infinite, ominous, fatally delightful hellspawn?
Have you tempted them with your divine belly,
such that they are even now rubbing it
to your satisfaction whilst forgetting the mortal world?
our gods have things to do
but there they are, standing at the sink to fill your water-bowl
(because the first flow of the tap is not worthy and they must watch
*with vigilance until the water you **like** emerges*
and meanwhile our prayers go straight to voicemail).

Hear me well, ye slaves of felinary: It could be worse.

Be glad that house cats are small, their claws capable only of drawing a little blood. Were they huge, they'd have no need for necromancy; they'd simply slay us all and then go seeking some other sentient race to give them obeisance. They would wait until the fullest moon and purrrrr in deadly unison until the vibrations reached out to that which is beyond the stars, and when the Ancient Ones arrived in this world to destroy it, those unholy things would, with their hideous misshapen mouths, speak:
"awwwww, how cute!"—
and by those words be damned.
Why do cats keep us alive? O foolish Zombies, *they never have.*
Still:
The house cat is but a tiger caged by its tiny frame, a thankfully miniscule skeleton stretched over the flesh of a

73

killer born. They are scritchable demons, playful, predatory, mouse-tormenting, catnip-seeking.

If you would see in this some horror, some internal disturbance at the black sorcery which plucked us from the tomb and made supplicants of our souls, be cheered. There are worse things in (un)life than subservience to such noble predators, creatures sharp of tooth and gleaming of eye. It's only natural that we worship them; and truly, who has the heart to chastise a cat? Be glad that they chose to strike us with some mysterious thaumaturgical enchantment, rather than simply using their claws to shred us like sofas.

When did they take our lives? I don't know, and I don't plan to ask; getting answers from Bastet is like putting a lion in a handbag: impossible, and probably unsurvivable. For you, not for the lion.

How did they keep us here, solid but enslaved? Oh, friends, surely, we enslave ourselves to our fears and our worries and our disquiet, every day; why should our relationship with *cats* be different?

A point, if I may. The puissance of felines reminds us of one of the cornerstones of magic, which is that the restrictions of your body are *not* the restrictions of your mind and soul. Your fleshly containment need not stop you from stretching your paws all the way from where you are, over and past spaces real and imaginary, straight up to the pillars at the end of creation.

Perhaps *you* must be a slave to your cat; but your mind needn't be a slave to *anything*. I don't know if they *can't* steal our minds, or if they just don't *want* to (or if I know, I ain't tellin') – but the point is, they haven't. Our thoughts are our own.

74

Villains, Villainy, and Villainpunk

Draw two lessons, if you would:

The reach of our consciousness may not be infinite, but it is vastly beyond the scope of our bodies alone. Let that make you *confident*; there are new places to explore, new possibilities to manifest, new mousetraps to build. And lest that make you *arrogant*, remember: no matter who you are, or whether or not you live with a feline yourself, you are permitted to exist on this plane *only* because somewhere, sometime, some cat thinks it may want the use of your thumbs.

Let's just be glad that there's plenty of sunbeams and balls of yarn out there to distract the beasts, and thus we generally have time to live *some* of our lives. Furthermore, they've let us stay conscious and upright (rather than, like most unliving things, flat and unmoving and thoroughly uninteresting to those who stalk the catnip) - and that means we must have *some* kind of future. We can't *all* die (again) in some horrible twist of fate, technology, or group madness. Because, if I may reiterate, it's clear that cats find us useful alive.

Of course, *sometimes* cats keep things alive just to play with them, and torment them, and watch them struggle *until* said cat has derived all possible amusement from the thing, at which point, it's lights out.

In my last conversation with Bastet, I brought up this possibility. I said, "We're still helpers, right? No matter how badly we treat each other, you're going to keep us around, aren't you?"

I'll never forget her reply. She said:

"Purrr."

"Purrrrr."

Jeff Mach

"PURRRRRRRRRRRRRRRRRRR."

The Huntsman's Story

O, Princess, when the Wicked Queen told me to bring her your heart, I could not. For what am I but the Huntsman? It's all anyone knows of me, and all I really know of myself. My craft is my name and my life. You were *too small*. That wasn't hunting, that would have been unadulterated murder, and would help neither Man nor Forest.

So I gave the Queen the heart of a wild boar; I suspect she guessed at the truth, but I prepared the meat carefully (over a fire of bramble and fragrant rare branches, using herbs few might find and fewer still might know how to use, roasted at the right heat and for the right time; how well a Huntsman knows patience!); and in the end, as is oft true of all but the most wasteful predators, the satiation of her hunger quieted her desire to kill.

And thus, she didn't chase the matter down. Not unexpected, really; once a pest is out of sight, it's natural to forget the thing, even if it isn't truly gone. If it troubles us no more, it can leave our minds; who cares what it does to the neighbor's garden, so long as it doesn't come back?

Now you *have* come back, and the Queen seeks you out, perhaps to slay you, perhaps to place you under some kind of Enchantment Unnatural. It's this latter I cannot allow. I am but a Huntsman; I can't predict sorcery the same way I might anticipate a heavy storm or an early thaw, and I therefore cannot protect that which I steward

77

from its unknown and strange effects. If I knew it would definitely be the poison, well, that's how one sometimes deals with pests; unfortunate, but understandable. But creatures of strength tend to *use* their gifts; a buck, who might protect his hard-grown antlers, might instead lower his head and charge, if the passion is in him. It is similar with the witch-born; sadly, my Queen has powers beyond those of most mortals (which, perhaps, reside also in you, her daughter). She might, in her anger, do something like raise up a maze of tearing briar, an invasive species which will seek water and nutrients from the soil and choke my trees; a tanglewood whose thorns will wreak havoc on the flesh and stomach of the beasts under my care. She might cause the palace, or even the Kingdom, to slumber for decades or centuries. Some of the naive think that if humans went away, nature would flourish, but humans are a part of nature, even when we do not cultivate the land or domesticate the beasts. Remove us, and our untended fields will invite blight or beetles, our carefully bred horses will lose their source of daily grain; and should lightning upend a tree and dam a river, or should drought overtake us, there will be no man-made solutions forthcoming. I have seen some of these things with my own eyes, when I traveled in my youth, and I have heard of it from those who came before me. This, *this* I cannot allow.

I could blame the Queen; but she's really only reacting to a threat to her ecological niche; that's normal. I could blame *you*, but that would be unfair. You were just a certain thing born into a certain place, and you never asked to be the progeny of a species which eats its own.

Villains, Villainy, and Villainpunk

To be honest, the forest doesn't care about either of you; it only cares about greenery and abundance, or disruption and starvation.

My mother, Huntsman before me, passed this down from my grandmother, who was Huntsman first of all:

"We can't always make the right choices for the woods; there's more to 'em than any individual can understand. But we can't stand idle, either. We try to make that which is under our care flourish, and grow as best we can, and sometimes that means nurturing a seed or a runt, and sometimes that means removing a threat with the most merciful shot we can manage. So, sharpen your eyes, sharpen your arrowheads, and do what must be done."

Perhaps you would defeat the Queen; perhaps she would best you. Perhaps you would be better for the forest, and perhaps you would be worse. You're an unknown, and my job holds too many of those already.

There is only one way to be sure of the disposition of your heart.

The Queen *seeks* you, but I *hunt* you; that's what I do. So, I'll get to you first. There's a family of boars who will consume anything I leave behind. When the Queen finds you gone, she'll be annoyed, but the fundamental problem will have vanished, and that will be enough for her. It always is. She never spends more time in my woods than she needs to; nobody does, for some reason. She'll go back to her palace and her mirror, and I'll go back to my cottage for a long winter's rest, nuzzling my kith and kin, and feeding on cold meat from the larder.

79

Jeff Mach

The Monstrous Meal of Tom Ramsey

You've perhaps not heard of Tom Ramsay; he's not the most famed of Villains, though I can assure you that he is quite a scandalous figure, and that has *meaning* in his social circle, where ill-repute is considered every bit as damning as, oh, say, human sacrifice. W. Somerset Maugham was kind enough to write about him a bit, and noted, among many other sterling qualities, the excellence of his table.

As is well-known, I was convinced, by certain persons who will not be herein named, to purchase a time-travel mechanism. After countless adventures, all of them quite horrible, I came to the conclusion that whatever powers exist out there, they *really, really* hate time travel. The only way to make *any* use of that particular phenomenon without opening up enough ill-fated potentiality to make a vengeful Djinn positively *hum*…is to summon its chrononautical abilities purely for trivialities.

So it is that I decided to travel back to the 19th century, wherein, upon presenting my credentials as a thorough cad with a penchant for playing baccarat and losing big, I was able to procure an invitation to one of Tom's little soirées. Being, as you know, the generous sort, I snagged the *cart du menu* for your edification, and I took notes.

You're welcome.

Dinner at the Lair of Tom Ramsay

Service à la Russe
Aperitif

Crème de cassis de Dijon avec Beaune Greves Vigne de L'Enfant Damien; Bouchard, 1864

(I was pleasantly surprised to note that somehow, Tom had gotten ahold of a Burgogne from, not before, but *during* the Blight. Impressive!)

Tom proposed what I later learned was his customary preprandial toast:

"Long life to all, and to any who, instead, die sudden and inexplicable deaths, your dessert is *mine*."

Soup Course

Potage a la Julienne. This refreshing, almost clear broth was, I am told, stock from the marrow of a fresh-shot Unicorn. I found my helping *delightful;* but the person next to me noticed a hoof in hers. The table roundly congratulated her, saying that it was good luck. This was true; in fact, it was *so* lucky that, before the bowls could be cleared, she was kidnapped by a Leprechaun. I finished her drink.

Salad Course

Jeff Mach

Salade Wyndham. Let me tell you, nothing cleanses the palate of the fear of vengeful Wee Folk like the discovery of **A BOWLFUL OF FRICKIN' TRIFFIDS**. Apparently, I passed out at this point. Fortunately, one of the guests was a physician, carrying the tools of his trade, and he applied a healthy tincture of Laudanum, then revived me with some *sal volatile*. The 19th century is GREAT.

Palate-Cleanser

Assorted Fruits of the Lost World. In honor of his successful conquest of the far-off land of Grover's Mills, New Jersey, Sir Ramsey served a selection of exotic drupes, including:

Sliced Passionfruit
Diced Crime-of-Passionfruit
Iced Dispassionfruit
Candied Cherries in Brandied Sherry and *Plums.*
(Technically, 'candied' anything is going to be too sweet to leave the palate neutral, I gotta tell ya, whatever you gotta do to make sherry into brandy, we should do it more often. I had a brief lie-down at this point.)

Intermède

Warmed Asparagus Spears. I missed these, being, as I mentioned, briefly non-upright. *They* didn't miss the person across from me, and servants quietly carried away the impaled body of our former companion. I began to realize that Tom is *serious* about his dessert.

I was revived by my good, good friend the physician, who injected me with a seven-and-a-half per cent solution. My heartbeat, which had slowed down to a pace more in keeping with geologic timeframes than human ones, now sped up in a manner similar to merry clip-clopping of iron-shod stallions as they charge towards you with an attacking Mongol horde on their backs. Refreshing!)

Fish Course

Angry Innsmouth Lobster. I had thought this a modern invention, but it seems there was a Ramsey family version which long predated the food fads with which I am accustomed. The Ramsey's tradition is that the seafood course be 'as invigorating as the sea itself', to quote Tom. These huge lobsters had been bred over the course of generations for sweet flesh and unbridled aggression. Tom waited until a lull in the conversation and suddenly loosed them upon us. He was kind enough to recommend that we arm ourselves with the medieval weapons which covered the walls; I had thought them to be decorative, but they were (fortunately) quite functional.

The resulting battle was pitched, bloody, and rather like something out of the Divine Comedy, and between the various substances in my veins, I'm not sure I would have believed any of it, if I hadn't taken a massive claw to the left outer thigh, leaving a scar I bear to this day. We, the survivors, with that fast and lifelong bond sometimes brought about by near-death experiences, feasted with

83

much joy, and then we plundered the bodies of the fallen for treasure, for such be the immutable law of the briny sea!

Accompaniment: Appreciative sips of an excellent Königsbacher Riesling 1827, served chilled in champagne flutes; and Grog, chugged.

Entrée

Un Cassoulet de Noachis Terra avec de herbes aromatiques. Of course, you are thinking: Mr. Wells has assured us that, while Martians obviously share some sort of biological compatibility with us (how else could they think to make use of Earth?)—they're not by any means meaty enough to be added to this most princely of peasant stews. While I would never cast aspersions on that learned gentleman, I'd like to remind you that he is known for his fictions. In point of fact, the meat, which had clearly been marinated in a bold Bordeux, was of a most exceptional mouth-feel, and held its own in this most robust dish, and quite fulfilled the Ramsey family motto, "Antequam comedam comedite".

Mignardese

Four and Twenty Blackbirds Baked In A Pie. Chef Anatole himself came in, and, in a Gallic accent thick enough to form a meringue, stressed in the *strongest* of terms, that blackbirds were out of season, and that he had, therefore, substituted a murder of Corvus Brachyrhynchos. After centuries of outwitting the semi-sentient scarecrows which dwell at the dimly-lit edges of the Ramsey estate, these

84

juicy and rapacious bastards are a treat to the diner, and a threat to all life on Earth. This year, *they're* in the pie; *next* year, things might be different. *Suggested Accompaniment*: Gin, swigged straight from the bottle.

Dessert

A selection of fromages de campagne, accompanied by wormwood-soaked cigars, because why the hell not, right? At this time, Lord Ramsay congratulated those of us who remained. True to his word, he consumed more cheese than I would have believed possible in man or beast, and seemed none the worse for it; I'm not sure, at this point, that he's even marginally human, and I have no desire to find out.

Finally, Tom offered us selections from the rest of his justly-famed wine cellar. He had recently acquired a cask of Amontillado from, he said, "someone who has no further use for it," and we washed that down with bottles and bottles of cold water imported straight from the River Lethe, but it was to no avail; *I remember every accursed minute of that meal.*

In good news, though, it turns out that Chef Anatole, while unable to pass into the next world due to his sins on Earth, and therefore technically a ghost, is fully able to wield kitchen implements with the same skills he employed while living. I dug up some of his bones (the Ramsay estate is now a shopping mall, and Anatole was living the hellish existence of a French culinary artist trapped in a food court), and he now inhabits my own abode. I'm having a dinner party next week; can you make it?

85

Jeff Mach

Under the Nether Bed

Stoned out of their *minds* on Hobbit blood,
Snorting dwarven gold,
Dragons getting the munchies,
Eyes bugged-out and rolled
From side to side in lizard slide
Stark with spark in threatening arc;
Wiggy as wizards and twisted as twine,
Penumbral beasts grown bored of myth
Beyond the barrier line.
What alchemy could burn a blood
That lives to father fire?
What herb or weed could fry a mind
That swallows souls entire?
Heat and steam and autumn gleam
Stoked and smoked, by blood invoked
Ticklish and tipsy and sordid and strange
Dwelling two inches inside your left ear
Beyond touch of time or change.

—And slapped by reality's cosmic broom..!
"*Shoo! Shoo! You nasty things!*"
Alien eyes glow crazed in darkness
Closet walls chafe green-scaled wings
Spaceless room and breathless tomb
Hid by lid and trap and id—
wished away by generations,

confidently thought destroyed,
they've found a hole
and they're
annoyed…

———————

I wrote *"Under The Nether Bed" in…1997, I believe. It was before I read Terry Pratchett's "Guards, Guards!", which (this is not, I think, a spoiler) also deals with the question of where Dragons* **really** *got to.*

I could definitely write a book or two of Dragon stories; but I don't know that it's what the world needs. Besides, not all Dragon stories are necessarily Villainpunk, and I think I want more Villainpunk in my life.

And I don't want to reveal too many of the secrets of Dragons. *They don't tend to* **like** *that.*

Jeff Mach

Of Goose and Gold

Once upon (a midnight dreary) there was a young couple who owned a goose, and this goose, in turn, laid golden eggs. I'm not sure exactly when the golden eggs came into the continuum. Had they just acquired the goose? Because the whole egg-laying thing can't have gone on very long before the meat of the story happened; otherwise, the story makes even less sense. (*Why did the goose lay golden eggs at all?* Why, because sometimes, there's *magic* in the world, and even when there isn't, strange stuff exists. We'll assume that this circumstance was unusual enough that the couple was extremely, extremely excited; but not *quite* so unusual that it led them to believe Armageddon was nigh, leaving them to flee, crying and wailing, out into the streets, wearing sack-cloth and screaming about the End of Days. We'll file it under "super weird, but hey, gold is gold".)

At any rate, this goose—let's say that they acquired it from a guy who knew a guy, with a whole bunch of other geese, and these people were at least partially supported by agrarian pursuits and the cultivation of livestock. Seems logical to you? Seems logical to me. Good.

—this goose just ups and starts laying golden eggs. Well, the first time it happens, the couple is astonished. Let's say it's a husband-wife team, and the wife person was gathering eggs that day. Okay, cue astonishment, comical dropping of a basket of eggs (all of which broke, except, obvs, for the one that was solid gold); a certain amount of shock and surprise; some kind of testing (I guess there was a village alchemist? We'll presume this took place at a time and place where you could get precious metals tested with reasonable accuracy, but the local government didn't have a monopoly on the good stuff. I'm having trouble picturing the historical era here, but really, history goes out the window when you bring auric oviparity into the equation, right?)

Okay, so, the goose lays a golden egg, it's real, the couple sells it, they're very happy, got it? Well, it keeps doing this for a couple of days, and they're basically in party mode. But they're also human, which means they want more. So they wonder, "How's a goose, being an animal, got all this gold inside it?— seeing as how gold isn't an animal, it's some kind of mineral or vegetable or something."

They think it out, and the conclusion they draw is, the goose must be full of gold on the inside, and it's moving that gold to the outside one day at a time. Now, here's the kicker: I don't know how big the eggs were, or how much a gold egg was worth, but these kids are *impatient*, so they kill the golden goose and slice it open in order to get at all the gold inside. Jokes on them! Ain't nothin' in the goose except, you know, goose stuff. No gold. The magic was somewhere in the *process*. And old Aesop comes in and points out the moral:

"*Don't kill the goose that lays golden eggs, ya morons.* Keep letting it lay eggs. Because it could maybe have done that forever and you'd have been rich, whereas now, you probably already spent your egg money on dumb stuff because first, you figured you were gonna have more gold, and second, you're idiots."

....and that's the story *they* tell.

But you know what *they're* like.

I wanted reality. So, *I* interviewed the husband.

Here's what *he* said.

"So, my wife comes out of the goose coop, and damned if she doesn't have another of those pieces of egg-shaped gold! They keep appearing on one of the nests, near this one real fat goose, my wife goes in every morning to get the eggs, and bam! another piece of gold. This has to have gone on four, maybe five days. Four days, five nights, maybe. Anyhow, fifth evening, I go to bed, I sleep, I wake up late at night, I'm hungry. We have a bunch of snacks, but nothing really satisfying. I feel ambitious, so I go into the coop, grab a goose, give it the axe, cook it, and eat it. Next day, my wife goes in to get the eggs and the gold, and the gold's not there. What the hell? First, I yell at my wife, because I figure she's just not looking in the right place, and she yells right back, and then we both look, and yeah, *somebody's taken our gold.*

"Now, I still had a piece left over that we hadn't spent yet, so I go into town and I get some guys and they build a hella big fence around the outside of the coop, spikes and everything, and just to be sure, I go to the apothecary and get something nasty and I pour it on the spikes, and one of the guys working on the fence starts complaining that it gave him a rash so I know it works, and they go home, and we go to bed.

Villains, Villainy, and Villainpunk

"And the next morning, we find out, it happened again: *some jerk's taken our gold*.

"And *it just keeps happening*. I call the cops, and they come by, but they're no good, they tell me there's nothing they can do, that there's no sign of forced entry, and also, they can put out an alert for any golden eggs that turn up on the black market, but they can't arrest anyone in connection with the non-appearance of spontaneously-generated precious metals. *Idjits*!

"So fine, I gotta do this myself. It's not comfy, but that evening, I sleep right in the goose coop. Well, I don't really sleep; those pointy-beaked bastards *peck* me all night. But I *watch* real careful, and there's not a sight nor sound nor hair (does gold have hair?) of that gold.

"So now I'm REALLY pissed! Some INVISIBLE jerk's nibblin' on MY gold.

"Maybe it's the Dark Lord. I hear we have one, two kingdoms down.

"Maybe it's the Bad Wolf, kicked out of the forest, making a predatory living.

"Maybe it's my wife.

"I up the security on the coop. And I take a bunch of straw into our bedroom—me and the ol' lady, we're not intimate anymore—and painstakingly I make a nest. 'Sit on it!' I order my wife, and dutifully, there she sits. It's very similar. Perhaps the original gold-givers will be deceived.

"Nothing's happened yet, but I'm patient. And this is what we do: we don't farm, and we don't raise animals, because we ain't stupid. That stuff's a sucker's game when we could be strikin' it rich with *our gold*. So we *wait*. Because we got priorities.

91

Jeff Mach

We will find the givers-of-gold and take their gold and find the takers-of-gold and take their lives.
And on-between, there's a lot of good eatin' left on this bird here.

This piece was originally much shorter; I had the idea of writing up the husband's story in a sentence or two and making the rest into a recipe for roast goose.

But it turns out that those recipes are really long, and also, this character just doesn't strike me as the type to prepare anything particularly interesting, culinarily speaking. I believe he's a bit more of a "pull feathers, make fire, burn self, curse, hold goose over fire, burn hand, pull goose off of fire, eat goose, burn mouth" kinda guy.

At any rate, as long as old Aesop's rolling in his grave, I'm happy.

The Sphinx's Last Riddle

I am the Sphinx. Once I was a statue. Now, I'm a woman, or a beast, if you prefer; now I'm something alive. Although I suppose that most who see me still assume that I'm inanimate, especially if they're looking from afar. No living thing ought to have a lion's body and a human face, which throws off first impressions considerably. It doesn't help that I don't always bother to move until I've a reason to do so, and (I will admit) there's a certain vicious pleasure to be gained in making mortals temporarily enter cardiac arrest when they realize that the stone thing is *alive*.

I am the Sphinx. They magicked me into life and told me to guard the crossroads. They told me to ask a riddle of any who passed, and to eat those who could not solve my riddle.

"What if someone comes with an army?" I wanted to ask. "I can't eat all of them, and I have no idea if I'm immune to catapults or battering rams. If you want to show off, shouldn't you protect your investment? I *know* I didn't ask to exist; why make me at all? Sure, this is a flashy piece of sorcery, but I can't believe it's the best use of magical time and resources. Oughtn't you save that kind of thing for problems which *can't* be solved through existing technology? I mean, standing in front of people and threatening them can be handled pretty easily with perfectly mundane methods. I can see all this making sense for some kind of lone spellcaster, because they don't have

93

armies, but you're not alone, and you *do* have an army. Couldn't you just put a garrison here, and if someone approaches, have a couple of burly sergeants take 'em into a little room and have the troops ask your question, and if the subject can't answer properly, it's arrow-to-the-chest time? It's not even like you'll be out the arrows; it's YOUR damn room. Pluck your bolts from the corpse and get on with things."

Is that expensive? Sure, but you run a nation-state, fellow. You've got soldiers already, and they're *practical*. THEY can, for example, send you written reports. Me, even if I could write, I got…paws.

And THEY don't have to eat their kills. Do you know how often travelers bathe around here? Not. Often. Enough. I bet you wouldn't eat unwashed *vegetables*, even; but *you* have a choice, after all.

These are the sorts of things I'd ask about if we spoke; but we never had that conversation. It was just ritual, ritual, ritual, spell, spell, spell, BANG! and I'm conscious, BANG! and I can move, BANG! "All right, here's a riddle, here's the answer, if they don't get it right, and they won't, gobble 'em down. I know they won't get it right, because it's my riddle, and I'm very clever." Then he pranced around a bit, admiring me, as I tried to figure out walking and such, and then he buggered off and left me here.

He can leave, no problem. Me? I've thought about it. Honestly, I'm not sure *what* happens if I try to move far from this spot. I'm not certain I won't just freeze back into unliving rock. If you've ever had a nightmare about turning to stone, becoming increasingly more rigid, less independent, less a living thing and more an object…then

94

start there, and now consider what that fear's like for *me*. I've *been* there.

If you want to know more about how it feels: Have you ever seen a statue and had a moment's irrational fear, "What if that happened to *me*?" Perhaps you'd focus on the interstitial, moment, that instant when the spark of life goes out. Perhaps you'd think the really bad part would come when you transition from living flesh into inanimate *objet d'art*. But *I know better*. I *know* that the spark of life goes out, *and then you just stay there, in whatever position you inhabited in the final instant of having any say in what happens to you.* And that's *all* you do: you *stay there*, slowly eroding in the wind and rain, for literal geological ages.

Sometimes, to give this particular horror just a little bit more juice, I've considered that the transformation might happen while I'm *flying*, and then I'd be Sphinx rubble, and thus, a tourist attraction. Maybe I'm wrong; maybe, if I tried, I could soar away free; but I doubt it. He told me to "stay", and, like a dog (I. am. *part. Lion. Not* the same thing)—like a dog, I stay.

Still, somedays, I'm frustrated enough to consider testing the barriers, to just run or leap as far from here as I can, except, except, except…

Someday, the person who gave me this riddle will return.

To check on me? To gloat? To renew the spell?

….to gloat, at the *very* least. There's only one person who knows the answer to this riddle, and he's it. And after a long-time of watching/meeting/eating people who think they're very clever indeed, I've realized:

Anyone who's more interested in being seen as smart than (for example) remaining out of my mouth…

95

….is a natural-born gloater.

So, I am quite certain: someday, he'll come back. To check his handiwork; to ask how many I've killed.

He's no fool, of course. *He* can answer the riddle, and I'm sure he'll be warded and guarded, and whatever magic made me will shield him from me.

Except.

Except.

Except:

I'm no longer a statue brought to life.

I'm a living, thinking thing who *once* was a statue.

He made me conscious—not out of kindness, but for the satisfaction of his own desires. He made me able to speak, the better the emphasize their failures. (More on that later.)

(I don't taunt them; at least, not unless they're truly arrogant in their own right. But I try to converse with everyone, before proffering the required conundrum. Some engage me; some toss pleasantries aside and demand the test immediately. My builder probably doesn't understand or care much about loneliness; I'm sure his own ego warms him at nights. But he never cared enough to limit what *I* might say, so long as, eventually, when those before me persisted in trying to pass, I asked the riddle before they did so. And then, of course, I slew them.)

But I've spent a lot of time talking to other beings. It's odd, to be popped into existence without much in the way of context. I know the names of, and can picture, all manner of things I'll never see; *snow* and *waves* and *forests*, for example. I've spoken much, and long, with seekers. Eventually, I began trying to convince them to turn around; eventually, some listened. It's not disobedience; my job is to prevent the passage of unsolvers, not to lure people to death. Sentients lure *themselves* to death; that's something I've figured out by now. Which was first confusing; having never wandered far from this single spot, I couldn't imagine expending the ability to go anywhere to approach, well, *me*, despite rumor, legend, and *so, so many bones in the sand*.

Eventually, it was enlightening. Choosing a path that will likely lead to death is probably not wise; but *that doesn't mean it's a bad choice*. There are things for which it is, perhaps, well-worth risking non-existence.

And it was with that knowledge that parts of me—parts unbidden, parts that were *my own*—began to come into being.)

Thus:

Let him command the parts of me that are a statue still; let him expect me to be lifeless stone unless he says otherwise; let him force my jaws to close and my mouth to shut, *if* he can. The *statue* was his. The Monster—*I*—well, *I* am *no-one's*, except, perhaps, my own.

And he'll find that out. I don't care if unmaking him unmakes *me* in the process; or, that is, I *care*, but I *choose*; I'd rather have *both* our deaths, instead of *his* freedom and *my* enslavement.

He gave me the ability to talk, and with that comes the desire, maybe a *need*, for a dialogue of some kind, even if it's only pleasantries or (sometimes) threats. And then he gave me orders which (eventually) end all of my conversations *quite* abruptly; and he, of course, never comes to speak to me. He never has. He never asked my opinion. Never told me his plan. Never gave me reason to believe I might *want* to do this, if given an explanation of why he wanted it done this way, and the choice to accede to the scheme or decline to be a part of it. He had the power to do any of those things, but so he *chose* to do none.

I have moved my own body, by myself, for myself, for so long; can he still it? I don't know if I have a heart; if I do, can he stop it? He made this mouth to speak, and to rend; can I turn it on him?

I'll tell you this: He'll need to get close to me, close enough to *riddle* with me. They *always* do; they always want to stay far away, but I always insist on a whisper until they come near. He *made* me, but he's no different from they; that's how he could craft them such an effective trap. I have met a thousand like him, many of whom could have found a way around me…but they didn't *want* to. Each *wanted* to be the one to solve the Riddle of the Sphinx; and nobody managed to realize she'd likely die trying.

This is the real riddle of the Sphinx: *Why am I awake?*

No, really. I could have been an automaton. There's only one correct answer to this question, or at least, only one that I'm allowed to accept; either they say the right thing, or they don't. I don't know much in the way of sorcery, but I'm pretty sure it would have been no less imposing for me to await the correct words, like a lock which fits just one key, and have me simply destroy anyone who gets it wrong.

So why did he make me a thinking being?

After many years of wondering, I'm pretty sure I have it. He wants me to hear each riddle, to think about it, to look sincerely at the speaker and say, "You are wrong." He wants them to *know* they're wrong, and to know that *someone else truly **heard** them, and **heard** them get it wrong.*

Why do I have a brain? *The better to spite you with.*

And that's why I know he's going to want to be very personal, indeed. I *could* have been a tool; but he *wanted* an unwilling slave. One who could think about running away. One who could see travelers coming and hate them simply *because they were allowed to be somewhere other than here*, even though *here* was where they were going, and where (bits of) their bodies would rest forever. He wanted a being who was conscious enough to give meaning to death after death after death.

So, I *know* he'll riddle with me. He won't just inspect me from a safe distance. Why would he? You don't simply gaze vaguely in the direction of your property and creation; you step on up to it and count its helpless teeth. I *know* he wants to look into my eyes, and if he wants to see my subservience—or my defiance—he'll have to be near enough that he could feel my hot breath on his face, if I had breath.

And when he gets up to my face, I'll *tell* him. *I'll tell him I'm not his anymore.* I'll tell him that if he'd had reason to do this, he should have shared it with me; that he could have made me an inanimate trap, or a living confederate, but I *won't* be some bastardized in-between thing. And then, by the Gods, I'll try to swallow him whole.

…and if he *can* really freeze me in place, if he *can* return me to what I once was, if he *can* make me a statue, it *doesn't matte*r. If I live, I'll eat him, and if I die—and this I swear, I swear upon the crossroads I guard, I swear by the mind that makes me what I am, I swear by the souls I've

99

Jeff Mach

sent to Hell with my words and my claws—if he kills me,
I'll *fall* on the son of a bitch.

Villains, Villainy, and Villainpunk

I Wake Down

I wake *down*.
In the chocolate insanity,
the sweet dark neverland,
I own a small but respectable burger joint.
My fare is decadent and greasy:
the fattening French fries of fantasy
the cholesterolic baconburgers of secret desire
the non-lite beer of childhood make-believe.
This is what I want to be.
An infiltrator pouring weirdness into the water supply.
A gremlin in the gears.
A toymaker, an eternal space cadet:
a purveyor of rhapsody
a whisperer
of wish.

Jeff Mach

Tao of the Closet Monster

*It's not an easy life, dealing with some interloper who thinks **your** bedroom is actually **their** bedroom. But that's just a fact of the hideous semi-life we call "existence". Here are some helpful thoughts to permit you to keep your peace of mind, even when you're just hanging out placidly in some closet, doing your own thing, and the nitwit in the bedroom drops a bunch of dirty clothes right on top of your camouflaged snout. Take it in stride and don't let it get you down; at least, not any farther down than you already are, you slithery thing, you.*

I. Remember: Others will try to shape you by filling your shell with hangers and clothing and sometimes bodies. Be unfettered. Emerge by night and streeeeeetch your sinuous body in the moonlight.

II. We might wish to chew up those who inhabit our foyers and clutter what is our rightful space with silly, pointless things like beds and desks, but remember: if you eat too many kids, your property values go down.

III. ...only they don't, really, do they? Chuck Palahniuk wrote some interesting things about this; I suspect he may have spent some time in the liminal spaces of closets or underbeds himself. He didn't quite speak the truth, which is why we let him live in (relative) peace. But in general, a smart realtor knows that there's an unending market for fools who will

102

never, even in the place of utterly meaningful and convincing evidence, believe unpleasant truths which contradict their worldview. They'll deny your existence right up to the point where you've swallowed them up to the thorax.

IV. With this in mind, why not partner with an ambitious salesperson of home and/or commercial landholdings? Oh, not every realtor is in league with Dark Forces, but the ones who are really ain't that hard to find, given a bit of effort. *Pro tip*: if you send the Lowerarchy a quick missive jotted on human flesh and worded with reasonable professionalism; they'll likely give you a helping hand. Or something very similar to a hand, anyway. After all, you're doing important work and bringing value to the local lack-of-soul economy. There's probably an enterprising young demon who can steer you towards some fool mortal, someone who has traded their immortal whatsis in exchange for transactional property-sale success, and from there, helping you source delicious bed-to-table gourmet monster comestibles is both a civic duty *and* a natural fit for them.

V. If things *do* get a little lean, take it in stride. Remember that we are, after all, supernatural, and while it's fun to crunch the living in your mouth-pincers, you can maintain a very happy and low-calorie lifestyle subsisting purely on a measured diet of midnight screams, with, perhaps, the occasional snack of whatever stuff in the kitchen contains the most sugar.

VI. *Don't forget to practice travelling rapidly from the back of one closet to another.* This is a big one. There are few things as embarrassing, not to mention inconvenient, as having someone say, "Look, there's no monster in this closet, I'll *prove* it to you," and having them push open your door and shove a bunch of socks aside, only to discover that their flashlight beam catches your posterior as you're morphed partway through a wall. The results, while temporarily hilarious, are always messy.

VII. Keep a stiff upper lip. Eventually, you'll have to have "the talk" with your interloper, especially if they've taken to annoying habits, like sleeping with the light on, or acquiring a suspicious cat. Humans are slow, and they're not the brightest stars in the galaxy, but eventually, you're going to set off their sixth sense at least enough to make them inconveniently uneasy.

VIII. So when the time comes, open the door of your abode, sit down on something comfortable (not the cat!), and stare at your interloper until they wake up. Sure, they'll howl uncontrollably (bonus!)—but gently shush them. Explain that *you're a figment of their imagination, and always have been.* They've been working too hard / letting school stress them out / not following their dreams / committing some other mortal sin. What they need to do is *relax*, understand that all nightmares end, and realize they're going to be fine. Have them repeat,

"There's no such thing as monsters,"

"There's no such thing as monsters,"

"There's no such thing as monsters."

104

Villains, Villainy, and Villainpunk

They'll forget you and sleep like rocks.

That's when you take a couple years off. Have a vacation. Hide behind some gravestones in a cemetery for a bit. Cross some stuff of your bucket list.

Then return to the mortal world, sniff out your interloper, find out what kind of closet they have now. Sometimes it's the same place, sometimes it's somewhere new. Either way, *go hide there.* I *know* you're hungry, but wait for your moment; if, say, they share a bedroom with someone now, wait until that person is visiting a friend, or out gathering green bits of paper, or whatever it is they do.

IV. *This* time, leaving the closet is special. Make it count. Classically, your big reveal involves phrases like "*Remember me?*" or "*I'm baaaaaack*", but that's a little passé, here in the modern era. Personally, I like to just stand there and smile big, *so big*, unhinging my jaw until they begin to realize that, in essence, closet monsters are nothing *but* jaws, with just a *bit* of sinuous body to accompany the teeth.

X. Their ear-piercing shriek makes *everything*, the wait, the travel, the emptiness in your belly, *all* of it, utterly worthwhile. And there'll be enough pulsating norepinephrine rushing through their limbic system to put a real *spring* in your step during your whole trip across town, all the way to the closet in your realtor's office.

Jeff Mach

A Pilfered Ignorance

(December 12th, 1887)

And now, dear Sir:

You have expressed to me on more than one occasion that you despise the literary device called "allegory"; that you cannot imagine how a well-reasoned thesis could ever be assisted by the introduction of fiction into the realm of the purely rational.

I don't intend to argue that point Sir, but I've chosen to answer your question with an allegory.

The choice of this device is purely coincidental, I am entirely sure, Sir. As always, I am careful to hold myself to a standard of behavior which is continually beyond any possibility of reproach. I am certain that no impartial observer, if any existed, would disagree. And you, yourself, are in whatever hole in the Earth has swallowed you; you are in no position, if I might say so, to evidence displeasure in my choice of literary format. Should you write me a rebuke, I will not take it as true displeasure, but simply assume that it is you, yourself, making excellent use of the many fine attributes of irony, whose understanding has been infused, by you, into my psyche with what I think we can agree is great success. What could possibly go awry?

(On a related note, I would be appreciative if you could arrange for another copy of the satires of Juvenal to fall into my hands; the reading library here is, shall we say, a little sparse in that regard.)

Though I suppose none of that will matter, should this missive reach the hands of authorities ecclesiastical. Should such a thing happen, please know, O learned fathers of the Church, that I am but a foolish girl, play-acting at the art of being an essayist, and I tell but the merest fairytales, of no more spiritual import than any story of enchanted princesses and speaking beasts of the field. I know not what I do. What female mind could conceive something as complex as a discourse on moral philosophy? There is no meaning here; I pray you, do not waste the time of your august personages in reading further. Consider the words beneath to have no meaning at all. Just stop reading now and send me back to the reformatory. There's no need for hot irons; I assure you, I have pre-emptively learnt my lesson; and if you damage my delicate person, however shall I work the laundry mechanisms, thus allowing me to be of some small benefit to the society which nourishes my iniquitous self?

(Oh, *thank* you, Sir, for ensuring that I consider the consequences of every action. You've promised me that only you will see what I write; but now I'm thinking about just what would happen if the Church *did* find some of these little notes. In completing even this, the first of your assignments, I note that I am embarking on a course of likely spiritual damnation and distinct physical danger. Have I mentioned how I appreciate your lessons in inductive reasoning? I haven't? No, nor shall I. Sir.)

And thus, to tonight's parable.

Jeff Mach

Once upon a time, the Gods decided to gift mankind with free will.

(As their existence far predated that of Mr. Hume, they didn't give it that name. They called it, rather, "choice," which seems a poor substitute; but linguistics is not our study tonight, especially as you haven't taught me any, Monsieur la Bête.)

Now, *why* would the gods want us to have "choice"? One theory is that they love us and want us to be happy. It is my understanding that this theory is particularly popular among idiots, who do not pay much attention to the world around them.

I have my own ideas, but I'll keep them to myself; there's no need to compound blasphemy with blasphemy, eh?

All right.

So the first to attempt to bring this gift to man was the God of the Sun. While he was not the one who originally crafted humans, he was perhaps the earliest deity to know their worship. Perhaps he felt grateful. Or perhaps, conversely, he thought they ought to be grateful to him, as he brought them light for their working days, and life for their agriculture.

He appeared in the center of the gathering-place of the tribe of humans, in the marketplace.

(Much could be said, Sir, about the state of humans before free will, and many questions asked, such as "How did they decide to form a civilization without self-determination? The anthropological considerations become sticky. Fortunately, this is an *allegory*, not a tale of natural philosophy. So I'll attribute to these antediluvian

108

persons some of the instincts of the humans we know today; let us simply say that they did, indeed, possess certain hallmarks of sapience, such as thought and discourse, but their belief in importance of individual thought and conversation was *even less than it is now.*

That idea threw me into three nights of malaise, and I was rescued from profound depression only by a practical understanding of the sorts of consequences I might incur if I was not, as instructed, finished with this assignment in a week. As you've put it, there are only three ways to fail out of being an apprentice cut-purse: bad death, worse death, or *extremely painful and lengthy* death.

I'm not saying that I think your assignment was a trap, but I will say that, after some consideration, I've decided that what the Gods were really attempting to force upon us was not "free will" itself, but rather, a mindvirus containing the *idea* of free will; that *believing* one's actions are one's own, and have meaning, and that one is not simply a clockwork toy or mechanism, trapped and forced to pursue a particular future because one has no other choice, create more possibilities than believing otherwise. This still doesn't actually prove that we *have* free will; but it does mean that those who believe themselves free will can, on a level playing field, accomplish more than those who believe themselves to be the slaves of Fate.

On that note, therefore, I'll continue.)

…The God stood proud, high atop a column of flame. All who looked upon him marveled; all would tell their children of this day. And he spoke to them, and said, "From this hour forward, all of you are free! You may choose to worship, or not. You may choose to act as you

109

please. Your movements are not predestined, and your fates are your own!"

The humans stood stock-still, motionless, as if afraid even to breathe. The Sun-God spoke again, a touch impatiently, "Go ahead, go and do what you think is best, based on how you see the world around you!"

Silence.

At last, the Sun-God said, "Speak. One of you, speak."

Tentatively, a man in the back raised up his hand. The Sun-God nodded to him. "O Lord of the Skies, Giver of Day," he said, "What would you have us do with this gift?"

The Sun-God smiled. "Anything you want. I simply hope you'll make the *right* choices."

The humans exchanged glances. Finally, the original speaker raised his voice. "Thank you, O Shining One," he said. "Would you kindly let us know which choices are the right ones?"

Speaking of, Sir—

I do endeavor to give satisfaction. I'm grateful for my placement in this...place; to quote another thing we used to say, back in my much-missed temporary home, it beats hell out of gettin' the hell beat out of ya.

But I've been up late the past three nights running, scribbling by candlelight in as fine a hand as I can manage, which, as you've noted more than once, isn't all that much. I figure, you're far away, and I don't even know how these pages will get delivered your way. Maybe they'll just languish in the drop-off place for a week, and here's me without sleep. I thought perhaps I might leave off here. I thought, what's the worst Monsieur la Bête could do to me, from far away.

Villains, Villainy, and Villainpunk

So, I didn't finish.

That's not the part I figured you'd be mad about.

You see, I dropped into slumber, and there, in my dreams, I was duly reproached.

But not by you, Sir, and for that, I duly apologize for a mind which scorns both the outer resource of the teacher and the inner resource of self-motivation. I appreciate your mentorship and your assistance, and I'd like to tell you that your firm instruction remains with me even in the dominions of Morpheus, but what changed my mind, what rose up from the land of Nod and brought about my completion of this task, well, it wasn't you. It wasn't my hopes for what a future might be, or even my thoughts of what I left behind.

It was Thief.

You'd have been proud. I looked her straight in the eye, and I said, in a heartfelt street patois, "I ain't afraid of you. I ain't got nothin' to steal.")

(My apologies for the grammar, Sir, but face to face with that personage, my demeanor may have lost a little of that hard-won polish.)

She cocked her head to one side, and I couldn't put her expression into letters. It was the smile of someone who knows there's something very funny, something you'd laugh at as well, if you only knew it, and if, when you figured it out, you could stop yourself from crying.

"*Don't make me steal things you don't even have yet,*" she replied.

And that's when I woke up, raced through my day's chores as if there were a dozen maids each clamoring for my job and every one of them a hungry hound of Hades, and thenceforth I crawled to the secret place in the basement.

Back, then, to the tale:

It takes great patience to keep the Sun on a straight path through the sky, day in and day out, and not let it deviate course except, obviously, to avoid the Star-Wolf. The Sun-God stood in the market for a long time, explaining that the entire idea was that the mortals make their *own* choices and not his. He was frustrated by their limited intellect (and, perhaps, his own; but what would I know of the limitations of shiny men?)

In addition, it is passing difficult for even our *own* churchmen to explain that we must simultaneously be obedient, and yet take responsibility for our sins. I would not like to be in the position of an immortal, faced, through a combination of certain metaphysical realities and a heaping dose of pride, with maintaining the idea that he *was* superior to those around him, but that, nevertheless, their choices *mattered.*

One might get certain ideas, Sir. One might, sir, question one's own inferiority. And how many superiors, in the depths of their chets, truly desire to hear *that?* The shinier the boot, the more the wearer wants to be sure who does the *wearing*, and who does the polishing.

Or so I have heard.

Eventually, with a long head shake of annoyance, he took off for the firmament.

In the mead-hall of the gods, the Goddess of Love looked patronizingly at the muscular figure whose chariot draws the Solar orb across the horizon of our little planet.

112

Villains, Villainy, and Villainpunk

"This calls for education. And...persuasion." Her friends cheered; the closer companions of his Heliotropic Majesty grimaced, and in a shimmer of the petals of some exotic pink bloom, the Goddess flew from the place of the Gods, to the place where mortals dwell, eventually alighting in the selfsame marketplace, astride a stallion of notably exceptional...stallionhood. A sort of symbol, you see, Sir. The powerful are awfully fond of such things.

If you're a mere human, surely it is life-changing to have one god appear before you. The second god is equally awesome, though perhaps just a tad less stunning. Humans adapt to precedent with remarkable ease. Or, as I used to say while sawing industriously at my bars with some laughably inadequate bit of stolen cutlery, "One can get used to near anything, if it doesn't kill you quick." Complacency, Sir; it sets in.

I can't speak much to the vagaries of fashion, but what the Goddess wore was red and flowing and timeless. She spread her hands, and the rapidly re-gathered crowd grew silent. They waited an uncomfortably long time; it might occur to one that the Goddess *enjoyed* being looked at and might have been a bit distracted away from what one might call priorities.

Eventually someone (was it the same one who'd spoken to the Sun-God?) asked of her: "What would you have of us, O Lady? What would you have us do?"

Smiling radiantly, the goddess replied, "I would have you do whatever you, yourselves, desire, o mortals."

What happened next would not, I believe have surprised anyone who's spent at least a year at Ms. Schrab's, or any other house of reformative justice in this great country, Sir, at least in my experience. The fact that it surprised the Goddess of Love suggests to me certain things about Love itself which are rather logical conclusions, if one makes inferences from such novels. (I hasten to report, Sir, that such things are the only literary materials available within this household. Please, Sir, I beg of you: *send books.*)

The Goddess watched the proceedings vantage point of height enough to make sure she was not entangled in the proceeding fistfight, and, eventually, she vacated the scene, with a certain urgency.

Her actions were not without longterm benefit for humankind, however. Even now, we remember the calendrical moment, if not precisely the year of this event, and the first day of May is well-known as a day when close interaction with certain of one's peers, particularly in the fields, is said to be correlated with bountiful effects upon the upcoming harvest.

In the halls of the Gods, there was argument. Perhaps "free will" was not of utility; would it, perhaps, be possible to replace previously-thinking beings entirely with amusing automata made of, for example, advanced building materials of the day, such as poorly-made bricks, or, perhaps, other, slightly-more-poorly-made bricks?

The Gods began arguing amongst each other; well, honestly, sir, more like a very angry droning. There was a church 'cross from Ms. Schraab's, and one had the opportunity to hear matters liturgical on a right regular basis. It's a bit of a personal belief that, were I the recipient of continuous and repetitive chanting, it might become a habitual matter of speech. It is for this reason that I have

114

endeavored to improve my vocabulary under your tutelage; that, and the Guild's generally-approved training method of ducking one's head in the water barrel any time one displays excessive ignorance.

At any rate, it was during the aforementioned Godly clamor that Thief, without word or ceremony, left the divine halls.

Now, Thief had another name at the time. She might have been the Goddess of some now-forgotten thing, perhaps. But that's not important. What matters is that, whilst the others argued, she made her way down to that selfsame marketplace.

She had no bright shine, nor any enchanting garment. It's not sure how she marked her own divinity, though I have a guess. It is sometimes said that we, her descendants, wear shadows as if they were cloaks. But Thief, now: *she* wore shadows like a crown.

Her divine nature was obvious to the onlookers, as it would have been to anyone. The questioning onlooker from before, having in one day communicated with major two Gods, was not entirely impressed with this rather-less-august member of the Pantheon. He asked, and it might almost have been a challenge,

"And what did *you* have to tell us?"

Thief smiled, that look which has made so many erroneously perceive us as wearing masks—when all we really wear is eyes which do not disclose the private matters of our heads.

"Nothing," she said. The onlooker replied, disbelievingly, "You lot keep coming on down here and behaving right mysterious. We've been around. You want something from us. What is it?"

Again, she replied, "Nothing. Nothing at all."

And thus, for the first time that day, a mortal spoke pure truth to the Gods.

"You lie!" he shouted.

This time, she didn't even speak. She only gave that smile again. It was an infuriating smile. It was meant to be.

A really dumb animal might attack its own reflection because it just isn't smart enough to know better. A human might attack *anything*, on account of being smart enough to persuade himself to do something *really* stupid. And besides, he was at the head of a crowd, and some crowds are only one idiot away from being mobs.

With a snarl, the man leapt towards her, and the rest of the marketplace followed. She twisted easily from her perch and fled…or at least, there was a chase, and she was in front of it.

Could she have lost them sooner? I think so. I suspect that with just the merest application of divine will, she might have dazzled them all into blindness, or disappeared, down to the last of Mister Dalton's atoms, in a single instant. And maybe even without powers, she could've shaken 'em all; she's Thief.

But that's not what she did.

Instead, she let them corner her, finally, in (for she's always been a traditionalist) a particularly dark alley.

They demanded, again, that she tell them why she came, what her message was, and she simply shrugged.

And then they tore her to pieces.

Villains, Villainy, and Villainpunk

This one took her brain, thinking he could capture her thoughts.

That one took her hands, thinking he could deduce her gestures.

Those took her blood, figuring it contained something special. *He* took her eyes and *she* got the got a hunk of skin, and

—suffice to say that every bit of her went to a member of the crowd.

And humankind spent a while in ghoulish contemplation of all the bits of Thief, thinking that if they could just recreate her, could just put it all back together in their own way, they would have the knowledge of the Gods, with no more evasions. As each little group tried to figure out what each piece might have done, they made a thousand guesses, they experimented, they fought and they argued and they went an uncountable multitude of divergent ways, until, at the end, Thief's body had been worn away to nothing by the abrasion too much human contact, and Mankind couldn't remember a time when we didn't have a legion of buzzing thoughts in our brains. And now, while many stay in their allotted slots and grooves throughout their lives, the world also turns up misfits, willing or otherwise: those who rebel, those who bite, those who question even after they've been ordered into silence.

This is the not-secret thing that Thief understood, and which, as far as I know, she never taught the Gods:

The Gods never gifted us with Free Will, because it wasn't theirs to give. It isn't anyone's to give. It can be found; it can be seen; you can lead someone to it, but you can't just hand it over. If you pour water on someone's face, they'll get wet; but you can pour knowledge into someone's senses all day long, and never touch the mind.

Thanks for tricking me into knowing that, Sir. I can't un-know it. I can't un-know consequence or my own responsibility for what happens to me, and I'll tell you right now: I hate it.

I can barely write a story, and you want me to control my own destiny? You're a right bastard you are, Sir, and that's the truth.

What happened to Thief? It's like I told you: *she* can steal things that aren't even there. So she robbed Nonexistence of herself. It took a long time, and it hurt like blazes, and there was no way to get all the pieces back where they were; but it gave her a chance to reassemble herself on her own terms. And *that* made it more than worthwhile.

WARNING: THIS ENTIRE BOOK IS A SCAM.

It's true. This entire book, the *whole* book, pretty much *all* of it, with the exception of a couple of numbers, is *nothing* but a whole bunch of *words*. *Seriously*. I'm really trying to foist that off on you: a whole jumble of locutions, just smacking into each other in a way which might, at *best*, produce a series of semi-indefinable, oft-intangible responses, such as feelings, thoughts, or ideas.

What a colossal rip-off!

And it gets *worse*. If you've read your Lovecraft, you'll note that there are generally two very, very important things about almost every single piece of writing he describes in his stories:

1. They aren't written by Lovecraft, and
2. They get you killed in horrible ways. (Or they drive you completely, unpleasantly mad.)

119

Jeff Mach

Here's a hint: I guarantee you that *this book wasn't written by Lovecraft.*

Need I say more?

* * *

And yet, there *is* more, because it gets *worse*:

I'm charging *money* for this book, even though *everything inside of it is available for free.*

That's *right*. I'm charging you for something that's *free*. Nearly all of this stuff is available on my blog *at no cost to you*. (This is even more ironic if you're reading this piece **on my blog right now**.) Oh, it would be a pain in the neck to go and find and click on each story, and this is a slightly-more-final edit, but I'm still an independent author who does his own editing, so it's not like we're taking a whole lot of difference.

There's even a very reasonable chance, if you're reading this, that you've already read most, and

120

perhaps *all*, of these stories. You've already put all the words into your head. Isn't that enough?

No. It isn't, *is it?*

Because there's still something about *books;* no, wait, something about *words.* Something that hasn't gone away, even though, in theory, the technologies of word-transportation have undergone fundamental alterations in their nature, not once, but many, many times. From stories spoken aloud, to pictograms carefully carved into rock, to manuscripts written out by hand and then copied slowly over lifetimes by rooms full of monks, to the printing press, to some kind of way the printing press probably changed that I don't actually know about but which was probably really important, to electronic books—there's still something that connects talesenders and talecatchers.

You shameful *hoarders-of-words.*

Face it. A certain percentage of those absorbing this information right now can't stop gathering mountains and mountains of verbiage into your

121

heads. Where does it stop? You're *worse* than Dragons; Dragons collect shiny, beautiful gold, with, perhaps, some rubies and emeralds. When most of the world's economy went electronic, did Dragons stop sitting on top of expensive metal and start metaphorically sitting on gigantic bank accounts? I don't know; they might have. It's not like they tell *me* these things. The point is, why are you still even *reading* this? This is a post full of words literally telling you to beware stuffing more words into your head and all you're doing is stuffing more words into your head and WHAT IS *WRONG* WITH YOU?

This Warning could end there, and it would, except that I am an honest huckster. And I should tell the whole truth:

I'm one of you. I'm a word-hoarder, too.

And I have some idea why.

There's something about developing stories and meaning out of stacks of language and communication which makes me feel more whole. Not like I felt incomplete before, but like there is *more* of me to be found, and I'm finding it and *making* it out of the raw stuff of thought and dream.

That's the conspiracy of writers: *words are never free*. Whether we are taking them in or putting the out or both, they cost us the skull-sweat and heartbeats and breath of constructing our dreamscapes, and for some of us, the more we add to those far-stretching inner skyways, the more our outside life has potential and joy.

If you like words as much as I do, then this warning is already far, far too late. Acquire these stories, *acquire all the stories in the world*, if you can. Sit your mind upon a throne of readable wealth so massive that even a Great Wyrm, tail sprawled lazily against a stack of emeralds each the size of skulls, haunches resting comfortably upon a bed of coins made from the treasure-troves of a dozen pirate-kings, would look at you, and envy your wealth.

Plunder and hoard, my ravenous story-kin. Plunder and hoard and good hunting to you all.

Jeff Mach

The Blighted Branch

(a counterspell)

And Blessed are those who have seen the Blight.

The tree has roots very deep in the soil,
but we've found a leaf with a bite of the Blight
(and Blessed are those who have seen the Blight.)

We'll cut it off, cast it into the night,
and so keep the tree well, and safe from the Blight.
(and Blessed are those who have seen the Blight.)

Although, *although*, if this leaf isn't right,
It could mean (it might, it *might*)
That there's a *branch* that's been blanched by Blight.

So to upper branches we'll swiftly alight
to check to see if vision bright
might note another touch of Blight
(and Blessed are those who've seen the Blight.)

Behold! It seems, it seems we were right;
Someone of most exceptional sight

124

Villains, Villainy, and Villainpunk

Has spotted a hint of the hideous Blight
(*and Blessed are those who have seen the Blight.*)

The tree is strong, and of great height;
The loss of a branch is a difference slight;
And it's well worthwhile to 'ware the Blight
(*and blessed are those who have seen the Blight.*)

...And now we've a moment of tangible fright.
Some of those with the excellent sight
Have spotted more Blight. *They have spotted more Blight*
On some branches we thought were totally right.
But now, to some eyes, when the sun's very bright
It looks like this we've found us some more of the Blight.
(*and blessed are those who have seen the Blight.*)

So off come those branches! But now, this fright:
Where else might be found the unseen Blight?
(*and blessed are those who have seen the Blight.*)

Something's wrong. Our chests are tight:
Why can't we better see the blight?
surely we should fix our sight,
so all of us can see the Blight.
And this thing, too, does not seem right:
They're not sleeping through the night,
The ones, the ones who see the Blight.
(*and blessed are those who have seen the Blight.*)

125

Jeff Mach

I think this branch might have the Blight.
(cast it, cast it into the night.)
I think *that* branch might have the Blight.
(cast it, cast it into the night.)
and now we've learned to fix our sight,
and now, we, too, can see the Blight,
and none of us sleep through the night.

If you even think it might be Blight,
cast it, cast it into the night,
For if you think it might be Blight,
I promise you, you're always right.
(and blessed are those who have seen the Blight.)

Learn from us this lesson bright:
We had some who didn't see the Blight,
and it turns out that they weren't right,
for some of those who had the Sight
realized: those people *were* the Blight,

and some we cast into the night,
and some suddenly saw the Blight,
and all realized (as well we might)
that nothing is ever safe from the Blight,
not once you've learned the proper sight,
the sight which knows how to see the Blight,
and we know everyone who's right
knows how, knows how to see the Blight

126

Villains, Villainy, and Villainpunk

(and blessed are those who have seen the Blight.)
(and blessed are those who have seen the Blight.)

now we cut away all that might
have ever been touched at all by the Blight,
and in solemn vow and rite,
we cast them all into the night.

But this is troubling. Everywhere my eyes alight
Seems to have a touch of Blight.
Surely that cannot be right;
But you die if you question the Blight, the Blight.
So either there's something wrong with my sight,
or *everywhere's* alive with Blight.

If the latter, no future's bright
not if everywhere is Blight.
And if the former, then the night
has swallowed up many who never had Blight.
(and blessed are those who have seen the Blight.)

(but that can't be right.
That *can't* be right.)

And now, none of us sleep at night.
Not fair. Not fair. Not fair or right.
We *cut* the branch, cast it out of the light;
So why aren't we freed from the bite of the Blight?

127

Jeff Mach

(and blessed are those who have seen the Blight.)
(and blessed are those who have seen the Blight.)

(...and Blessed are those who have seen the Blight.)

128

Unsacred Band

"And I accept your pledge, with gratitude, Knight; be welcome. I do try to greet new recruits, especially those of your reputation, but I seldom have much time for talk. So, while you're here: have you any questions?"

The Knight paused a moment, waiting for a formal command to unbend his knee; but the General simply lifted her hand in a "get up" motion: a polite but most *in*formal gesture. This suggested she cared more for practicalities than niceties, which was a very hopeful sign. That much, at least, matched what the Knight had heard, when he first set out for this place. He shrugged internally (why telegraph the language of your body if you don't have need?) and made up his mind. Now was as good a time as any to find out if the *other* rumors were true; she'd invited inquiry, and if she didn't really mean it, best to learn that *now*, with a sword at his side. As usual, his thought-stream divided things into strategic possibilities: if this court were as touchy about *lèse-majesté* as most he'd known, he'd find no happiness here. He'd have another price on his head for insult—which is to say, honesty—towards another crown.

And there were no other kingdoms left; this was a last resort. So, if what he was about to do was idiotic, then it was, at least, logical; better to do it armed and ready than let it happen at some less-chosen moment. Who wants to die like a fool in the middle of some pointless social function, dressed idiotically in the finery of the ballroom,

naught but a little ceremonial knife at your side? Right *now*
he wore armor; right *now*, he was near a foe of meaning,
and if there was a clash, it would be of arms, not of the
colors of courtly attire. And at least this way, his life would
be sold, not taken.

His peripheral vision was not excellent, but it was, like
any part of him which had to do with matters of combat,
both trained and disciplined. He used it for a final look at
the guards (why let them know you're looking at them? If
they're not smart enough to guess, that's on them.) He
approved: they were alert, and in sufficient numbers to take
him, which was appropriate, since he'd not yet earned real
trust. The combatants he saw were clearly strong enough
to do the job, but he was strong himself. If he was about to
commit treason, he'd stand no chance; but he reckoned
he'd take one or two with him. That was good enough.

He shrugged again, but this time, he let his shoulders
move. He wouldn't be able to keep the uncertainty out of
his voice regardless; let them think it might be a symptom
of fear, which was a weakness, rather than knowing his
actual weakness—namely, that he was permitting himself to
hope.

He took a quiet, very even breath, readying his voice
for speech and his limbs, should they be needed, for
motion. He looked up at the tall figure, past the telltale
brand on her neck, and met her gaze.

"General, everyone has told me that you're reluctant
to speak of your own past, so I won't ask it. However, I
have a question that's close enough, and I apologize for
what I realize is a breach in protocol."

Villains, Villainy, and Villainpunk

He didn't have to look, not even with the corners of his eyes, to feel the fighters around him tense up. But the General's tone was neutral and controlled; he couldn't read it. "Go on."

There are entire arts of war built around simply drawing a sword with more rapidity and decision than an opponent; and they are most practical. Unsheathe too slowly, or with too much hesitation, and you likely die. But draw and cut unwisely, roll the wrong head, and, *again*, you will die, and perhaps those you protect will perish *with* you. Speed, decisiveness, proper action; those are hallmarks of one who could survive more than one battle. And this made him even more aware of the long silence in which he stood, like a statue of a warrior, unsure how to frame the next (his last?) words.

Finally, he just opened his mouth and let the words tumble where they would. "General—Commander—I know why I came here. I was cast out by those I served, and I'm grateful to be accepted. But…" He felt his face grow hot. Why hadn't he paused a little in his training to study diplomacy? …oh, he knew why. He'd had contempt for those whose tongues formed poison and honey in the same breath. He'd thought them incapable of real action, right up to the point where they tumbled him from his place.

And landed him here.

He took a step forward. Her closest guards put hands on hilts; he heard the familiar click of a blade unshipped, but not yet pulled. Didn't matter; he no longer cared.

"I'm sorry, General. I've just heard too much. I will be serving with these beings, and I *must* know who's to be at

131

my side. Some say they're formed from dragon smoke;
some say they're demons; some say they're warriors
possessed, or...or even the dead, brought back through
arts beyond my understanding. General! I do not accuse
you of any impropriety. All have some idea of what it cost
you to be where you are now; and I have already sworn
you my life. Whatever strange arts brought you this army, it
is *my* army now. I care not what manner of things they are.
I swear; I am a simple man, and the ethics of the battlefield
are enough for me. Just tell me—" and it was good that
emotion had taken him now, as, had he been thinking
clearly, he would have been ashamed at the way his voice
broke, something it had not done since he was a literal
child. Now it became a whisper. "Tell me, my General and
my Liege...with what sort of creatures have I cast my lot?"

He tried to force himself to wait for the answer, but
both mind and body disbelieved. *No on*e would tolerate this
level of impudence; he'd gotten it all wrong, there was
probably some protocol he'd never even considered; if he
were going to ask, he should have asked another way...

He half-drew his own sword, expecting to hear the
weapons of his almost-companions clearing with two
dozen metallic rasps—

All he heard was laughter.

Laughter from the General; and though the
regimentation of the soldiers (he noted, with professional
approval) remained perfectly in place, he'd been a fighter
far too long not to recognize crinkles in the eyes of even
the sternest battle mask. The laughter felt *good*; felt like
what you'd hear around a campfire, at the end of a long
day, when no-one thought too much of rank or title, they

just cared they'd survived. And the General's mirth had a ringing quality; he'd never heard it before, but he thought he could identify it. It was a sound a throat might make if once, it had been cinched to a tight iron collar. It was the laughter of someone who had burnt off her shackles; and then made sure that those who shackled her would never, ever do so again.

And she smiled.

"They came as you did, good Sir Knight. Cast out. As you were. As I was." She paused, then looked about the room. "As we all were."

At this, he lost control.

There was no excuse. He knew he was no smooth-talker, no diplomat, *but he was supposed to have a damned grip on his ten-times damnable tongue.* And yet, the words tore lose, far too quickly for him to muzzle himself. It was barely communication. It was sheer *disbelief.* It was also **suicide**; what he'd done already was very, very risky, but this was outright madness. It requires no expertise in etiquette to know: *You don't call a ruler a liar in her own throne room.*

Didn't matter; the outburst pried itself out from his mouth before he could move to hold it in:

"That's impossible!"

What flashes before a true warrior's eyes at the moment of death should not be, as popular myth would have it, his life, but rather, a clear view of the flurry of blades which are about to cut him down. For even in its final instant, the strategist's mind should not be absorbed by fear or self-pity or even the pain; it should marshal every fragment of resources, and seek a way to inflict one final, terrible wound on the remaining foe.

None of that happened here. The atmosphere in the room had changed, but it wasn't hostile; if anything, it felt…sympathetic.

He was suddenly unsure what to do with himself; a man of perfect balance now seemed ill at ease even standing still. In search of some action, any action whatsoever, he took a few steps in the direction of the north wall, near a window. The Keep was tall, with its viewpoints carved sensibly high, well beyond easy range of most missile weapons. He looked through the nearest arrow slit, through which his practiced glance could take in the Army beneath. As he'd ridden in, his mind had quietly catalogued weapons, armor, estimated numbers, and, most of all, taken some measure of the creatures he saw. If they looked oddly human, that's because it's what they *were*. They *also* looked tougher than most with whom he'd ridden in the past. These were blooded veterans, forged rough and hard like the iron nails of a Faerie coffin. And they were vast in number, *so vast*; they covered the land as ice covers a demon's heart.

The Knight turned his head back, once more, to the General. 'But—but who would cast out so many of their number, thus *freeing* them, hardened by the gauntlet of banishment, to create an implacable foe where there's hitherto been none?'

The General smiled. Contrary to legend, her teeth were not fangs, but if she'd had them, they'd have been right at home in the expression her face now bore.

"Fools," she said quietly. "Fools who are likely to die."

The highest window in the room held, at the periphery of what it made visible, the faraway lights of another force,

134

an even larger one than their own, perhaps two days' ride away. And getting a little nearer by the moment.

"All those souls," he mused. "All of them ready to fight whatever we might be—hellspawn, lizard magic, corpses, anything."

"Yes," she said. "Now that they see who we are, they'll throw anything at us to keep us from coming back."

Again, he looked up at the tall woman, not thin, not old or young, whom he now served. "And will we?"

"Come back?" she replied, her face to the window. She turned. "I'll make *that* decision from the highest vantage point of a wall, formed of the corpses of those who tried to make the decision *for* me."

The Knight smiled. For the first time in his life, he was home.

Jeff Mach

The Frog Variations (A Fairytale Gone *Quite* Awry)

I. *The Witch stayed around for a final drink in the tavern.* She told a big truth—*Magic could transform humans into frogs!* There was also a bigger lie: *a kiss could turn them back.* She might have suggested both things had happened. More than once.

So the townspeople slowly, night by night, trickled to the pond, in search of the frog-snog that leads to possession of half a kingdom (or more) through a Royal marriage. The fact that none came back was taken as proof of the efficacy of this plan; the water was probably just *full* of aristocrats, and all the lucky townspeople were either journeying towards the fabulous wealth of some other kingdom, which had long been missing its noble heirs; or else enjoying some exquisitely drawn-out honeymoon in assorted exotic locales.

So, they crept to the murky water in ever-increasing numbers, now two per night, now three, now a new one pretty much on the hour. It turns out that the less greedy, seeing everyone else apparently vanish into luxury, became just a wee bit *more* greedy. And when so many were making the pilgrimage that they began bumping into each other, such that the transformation happened in full view of others, *each* thought, "Well, there was clearly some inherent wrong in *that* person, which made things go haywire; it won't happen to *me*."

Villains, Villainy, and Villainpunk

That did not, in the end, prove to be true.

Ever-more-numerous were the transmogrifications. If anything, people thought that the problem must lie in insufficient eagerness, or a deficiency of faith, and they began, quite literally, leaping into the pond in a frantic surge of osculation. Now it is a kingdom of frogs, all fighting each other constantly for a mouthful of flies.

II. *Or perhaps*:

What's more compelling than the thought that some simple act, something momentary and simple, if unexpected, could make you rich, rich, rich?

The thought that there's an *awful, horrible secret* somewhere in the mix.

Come *on*. If all the townspeople knew that the Royal spawn has gone amphibian, surely the Palace knew it, too. Why wouldn't the rulers send some high-powered cursebreaker, some specialist, some of the sort of extra-potent help you can only get when you're loaded with loot and command a reasonably large standing military?

Clearly there was some kind of scandal. Somebody *wanted* that froglet to stay a froglet. But what could it have been? Was it an improper liaison with an Elf? A murdered political rival? Was it possible that the entire Royal family had *always* been cursed amphibians, and everything else was just a front?

Sure. In a world of magic, why *wouldn't* it be possible? The allegations abounded. Everybody believed; believing the worst is pretty much what humans *do*. But people were a bit divided in their responses. Some wanted to laugh. Some wanted to weep. And a few wanted to help.

Jeff Mach

The kindest of the kingdom, the people with the greatest desire to care for others, the ones who most tried to see the good in others, began to make their way to the pond. Soon, as the most compassionate of the kingdom, those who'd most want to assist in breaking an evil enchantment, began to disappear, it was the most self-centered, the least helpful, the, let's not put too fine a point on it, *worst* people who remained, well, people.

And those folks had many offspring, each one brought up by those with the *least* empathy. It was a kingdom of narcissists and sociopaths—and it is *your* birthright now, Princess.

III. …but *actually*:

Actually, the frogs all left the kingdom in haste. They knew something important: No matter *what* the story is, once they kiss you, *you never, ever get the taste of human out of your mouth.*

Coyote is Not Real

One day, Coyote decided to steal pretty much everything he could get his paws on.

He went to a vast lake and saw the moon on the surface of the water. "I know what you're thinking," said the Moon, "and you cannot do it. For I am but a reflection of the Moon. I appear to be a beautiful pearly circle, so close you could just snatch me up, but if you tried, you would merely swipe right through me, disrupting the very image you love. And if you kept trying, you would eventually overbalance and land right in the water and go home, empty-handed and soaking wet. In a way, it's a metaphor—"

And it cut off abruptly, as Coyote plucked the Moon out of the lake and popped it in his sack. And on he walked.

Next, Coyote decided to steal the Sun from the sky. Perhaps this was a kindness; after all, the Sun and Moon live together in the house which is the firmament, but they never get to see each other, for each must make appointed rounds at immutably disjointed times. The Sun was on the other side of the world at that moment, of course, but Coyote had a trick:

You know how, when you are very tired, sometimes, you close your eyes, and you're sure it only lasts a moment, but just when your dreams are getting really good, the Sun's bright rays awaken you? Coyote spent much of his

139

time perfecting the magic of dreams (or, as Grandfather Crow called it, "Loafing around like an aimless galoot"); and so he somnambulated a truly great fantasy (it was about a peanut-butter-and-banana sandwich taller than he was). He was still trying to figure out how to get his jaws around it when, sure as meat loves salt, a sunbeam splashed across his face. Coyote can be clumsy, but sometimes he is very quick; before his eyelids even finished opening, he grabbed that sunbeam and *yanked* in a special way, and bam! the Sun joined the Moon in the sack.

(It took *excellent* aim to get it straight into the opening of the bag; *clearly*, the long days he had spent popping morsels of food into his mouth without looking had been *valuable practice*, and Coyote was, once again, proven extremely wise.)

Then Coyote thought he might steal all the Stars; but the Stars, not having born yesterday, saw what happened to the Sun and the Moon, and they'd already left, going on holiday to faraway Kalgash; but that's a different tale.

Coyote then wanted to steal the secret of Wine from the Gods, but as he approached the celestial Tavern, he saw that the bouncer was looking at him with recognition. The Bouncer spoke words of power ("You gonna pay your tab?")—and Coyote fled.

Coyote then stole all the left socks in the world. Why the *left* ones? Well, why not?

And at last, Coyote decided he would thieve the greatest treasure of all, Knowledge. So, he searched out the biggest University he could find, and there sought out a Professor of anthropology. Boldly Coyote stepped right up to him, thinking of clever and crafty schemes.

140

Villains, Villainy, and Villainpunk

Before Coyote could open his mouth, the other spoke. "You don't exist," the Professor said.

"I most certainly do!" said Coyote, startled out of his plotting.

"No, you don't," the Professor replied. "Lots of peoples all of the world have lots of Gods. The reason for that is, humans are basically primitive and superstitious. They make up stuff to help explain the world because they don't understand how things really work. So they create, say, a God of Lightning because they don't understand that the big flash in the sky is just a meteorological phenomenon."

"I see," said Coyote. "And how *does* lightning really work?"

"Electricity," replied the Professor. "Clouds. Ion particles. Superconductivity. Not my field, really. But anyway, I know there's a perfectly natural explanation, and that's better than Gods."

"Better how?" asked Coyote.

"Well, if somebody knows how electricity works, they can make machines which use it. Whereas if somebody prays, who knows what will happen?"

"Is there some particular reason why a God of Lightning wouldn't fit electricity into some reasonable framework of the way the world works? It seems to me like that would make a lot more sense and be a lot more viable than needing to make a conscious effort in order to permit every single individual spark to ignite. And obviously Gods don't always answer people; that's hardly proof that they're null and void. Are you caught up on *your* email, Professor?"

141

Jeff Mach

The Professor shrugged, annoyed. "I happen to be religious, like many anthropologists; but that's *personal*. I can believe, for myself, that God or Gods are real; but I'm hardly going to believe that some *particular* god takes a physical form and knocks on my door in pursuit of some kind of myth-fulfillment. I don't care if you think you can justify *your* existence; the point is, if anthropologists went around saying, 'So-and-so people believe in such-and-such a God because that God is quite real and will be annoyed if they don't believe', nobody would take us seriously. We wouldn't be a science."

"Wait a minute," Coyote said slowly. "So, you're telling me that your entire field of scientific endeavor needs to disbelieve in me, or you'll lose your own credibility?"

"Of course."

"So…no matter what I do, you'll disbelieve in me, *and* you'll tell everyone else to disbelieve in me, and the more firmly you describe me as an illusion, a folk tale, a primitive metaphor, the better off you are?"

"Of course."

"But I'm standing right here. In front of you. I can tap you on the shoulder. I'm quite real."

Coyote prepared to begin doing all manner of things to show that he was a material being occupying the same plane as the Professor, but the Professor held up a hand. "Anything you do could be a dream, a hallucination, a false memory, or, if worse comes to worst, something I can't explain, but which I *know* cannot possibly be *you*. Whatever you do, I'll ignore it, and so will every other right-thinking person. I *know* you're not real; my friends and companions know you're not real; you're not going to change my mind.

142

Villains, Villainy, and Villainpunk

I'd have to rethink just about everything if that happened, and I'd be on my own in doing so. I'd be shunned, laughed at, scorned. So, get used to it. *You are not real.*"

The beast stared at the man for a moment. Then, with unusual humility, he walked forward and extended a hand. The Professor took it. "I'm sorry about this, but there's nothing I can do," said the Professor. "No, no," said Coyote, "*Thank* you."

Coyote walked carefully out of the University. He pawed into his sack, made sure the Sun and Moon were comfortable and the socks all stored as efficiently as possible. It was a big sack; there was still plenty of room.

Coyote took a long look at the big, sprawling idea-factory which was dedicated to proving that he wasn't there. He smiled a slow, wide, Coyote smile.

Then he stole the world.

Jeff Mach

THE END.

Made in the USA
Middletown, DE
23 January 2020